POVERTY IN AMERICA

POVERTY
IN
AMERICA

WHAT WE DO ABOUT IT

BERTHA DAVIS

Franklin Watts
New York   London   Toronto   Sydney
An Impact Book   1991

Graphs and tables by Fine Line Illustrations

Photographs courtesy of: Photo Researchers, Inc.: pp. 24 bottom,
37 bottom (all Spencer Grant), 24 top (Ed Lettau), 25 top
(Herman LeRoy Emmet), 37 top (Katrina Thomas), 41 (Catherine Ursillo),
64 (Barbara Rios), 78 (Bruce Roberts); UPI/Bettmann Newsphotos:
pp. 25 bottom, 30, 53, 69, 85, 96, 112.

Library of Congress Cataloging-in-Publication Data

Davis, Bertha
Poverty in America / Bertha Davis.
p.   cm.—(An Impact book)
Includes bibliographical references and index.
Summary: Examines the living conditions of Americans from the
lower economic classes and briefly discusses programs intended to
assist them with their financial burdens.
ISBN 0-531-13016-9
1. Poor—United States—Juvenile literature.   2. Economic
assistance, Domestic—United States—Juvenile literature.
[1. Poor.   2. Poverty.]   I. Title.
HC110.P6D375   1991
362.5′0973—dc20   90-22622 CIP AC

CONTENTS

POVERTY IN AMERICA

PREFACE

*The greatest of evils and
the worst of crimes is poverty.*
—*George Bernard Shaw*

Even those who might question Shaw's superlatives are unlikely to reject the challenge his words imply: the human misery that poverty causes is an evil; the existence of poverty in a society that could eradicate it is a crime.

During the 1930s, as President Franklin D. Roosevelt embarked on his New Deal programs, he spoke of the one-third of the nation that was ill-fed, ill-clothed, and ill-housed—in other words, the one-third that lived in poverty. By 1960, owing partly to Social Security and mainly to the expanded job opportunities associated with World War II and its aftermath, the poverty fraction had dropped to one-fifth. But in the judgment of Presidents John F. Kennedy and Lyndon B. Johnson, there were still too many poor people in the richest nation in the world.

Thus, inspired by the accomplishments of the civil rights crusade and spurred by the writings of Michael Harrington, Kenneth B. Clark, and John Kenneth Galbraith, the 1960s witnessed the declaration of a War on Poverty, a foundation of social legislation to reduce poverty on which presidents and Congresses thereafter have built and continue to build.

Today, more than twenty-five years later, poverty persists in the United States and we must ask ourselves why. How have we responded and how are we responding to the challenge presented by continuing poverty? Those questions are the focus of this book.

1
WHO ARE THE POOR?

Poverty, says one dictionary, is "the condition of being poor with respect to money, goods, or means of subsistence." Which raises the question: What size income makes one "poor with respect to money"?

HOW WE KNOW WHAT WE KNOW
ABOUT POVERTY

In 1988 the population of the United States was about 243,685,000. These 243.7 million people received money income totaling about $3,197,878,255,000.[1] These numbers come from the Census Bureau. Everybody knows that the Census Bureau collects information about the people of the United States every ten years. Less well known are other data-collection activities performed by the bureau to keep information needed by government and business up to date.

For example, in March of each year the Census Bureau carries on a Current Population Survey (CPS). In March 1989 interviewers visited about 58,000 households and recorded detailed information about the individuals in each household, their work and education experience in 1988, and the money received by the household during that year. The 58,000 households are a so-called *representative sample* of the nation's population. That is, they are selected by expert statisticians in such a way that data about them can be expanded ("extrapolated" is the technical word) to yield an accurate, detailed picture of all the households in the nation.

The 58,000 households in the sample were drawn from the 1988 total of 92.8 million households. Of that total, 65.8 million households were families, defined as two or more persons related by birth, marriage, or adoption and living together; 22.7 million households were individuals living alone; and 4.3 million households were two or more unrelated persons living together.[2]

CPS findings are published in the Census Bureau's Current Population Reports. All the data in this chapter are from a report on findings from the March 1989 Current Population Survey, the most recent such report available while this book was being written.

HOW THE NATION'S INCOME WAS DISTRIBUTED IN 1988

The $3.2 trillion aggregate income reported for 1988 included income from all sources: wages and salaries, interest and dividends, rents, pensions, public assistance (welfare, for example)—in other words, any money payments regularly received. If that $3.2 trillion had been divided up equally among the nation's 243.7 million people, each individual would have received about $13,120. That number is what is called the nation's *per capita* income. Of course, in reality there was no such equal distribution.

How does the Bureau find out how the $3.2 trillion was actually divided among the nation's households? Basically, something like this goes on: Imagine a computer-produced list of the income received by each of the 92.8 million households; the list starts with the highest household income and proceeds in descending income sequence. The computer then divides the list into five groups, each called a fifth. It computes the total income for each fifth, then computes what percentage each fifth's total represents of the $3.2 trillion aggregate income. Figure 1-1 shows the result in 1988.

Bear in mind as you look at those percentages that each fifth had the same number of households. The 18.6 million households who fared least well shared 3.8 percent of $3.2 trillion; the 18.6 million households in the top fifth shared 46.3 percent of $3.2 trillion. You can see how these figures point to a very unequal distribution of income.

Figure 1-1. Percent Distribution of Aggregate Income (1988)

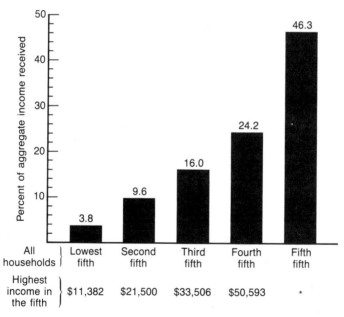

Source: U.S. Department of Commerce, Bureau of the Census, Current Population Reports, Money Income and Poverty Status in the United States: 1988, Consumer Income Series P-60, No. 166, p. 31.

THE POVERTY THRESHOLDS

All this is essential background, but the answer to the question posed by the title of this chapter—who are the poor?—has not yet emerged. There are households in the lowest fifth who are not poor and households in the third fifth who are poor. Why? Because the United States government uses what is called an *absolute* standard to define poverty. It says, in effect, that a family of four—mother, father, two children under 18—whose income is less than $12,092 is poor. This family is below the poverty level. A woman aged 65, living alone, whose income is below $5,674 is poor. A mother, father, and five children will live in poverty unless the family income exceeds $18,248. In other words, *poverty thresholds* determine who is poor and who is not poor.

The story behind the poverty thresholds is interesting, especially because some believe the thresholds are not completely satisfactory determinants of poverty status. In the 1960s the Department of Agriculture developed an Economy Food Plan, the lowest in cost of four food plans designed to meet nutritional standards at different income levels. An earlier study by the department had found that families of three or more persons spend one-third of their incomes on food. So, it was reasoned that the cost of the Economy Food Plan, multiplied by three, would indicate the minimum income on which a family of three could be provided with food and other necessities.[3]

The Census thresholds shown in Figure 1-2 were computed using the formula given above. These thresholds differ from year to year because they are adjusted to reflect changes in prices. For example, in 1987 the threshold for a family of four was $11,611; in 1986 it was $11,203.[4]

In administering the poverty programs that will be described later in this book, the Department of Health and Human Services uses poverty income guidelines that are

14

Figure 1-2. Poverty Thresholds in 1988

Size of family or household unit	Threshold
One person	
16 to 64 years	$6,155
65 years and over	5,674
Two persons	
Householder 16 to 64 years	7,958
Householder 65 years and over	7,158
Three persons	9,435
Four persons	12,092
Five persons	14,306
Six persons	16,149
Seven persons	18,248
Eight persons	20,279
Nine persons or more	24,133

Source: U.S. Department of Commerce, Bureau of the Census, Current Population Reports, Money Income and Poverty Status in the United States: 1988, Consumer Income Series P-60, No. 166, p. 88.

very similar to, but simpler than, the Census Bureau's thresholds. For statistical purposes, however, it is the Census Bureau's poverty thresholds that define poverty. It is the bureau's poverty rate and other poverty data that are released to the press.

POVERTY IN 1988

When the Census Bureau's thresholds were applied to the incomes received by households in 1988, these official poverty figures emerged. The number of persons who lived below the poverty level was 31,878,000, or 13.1 percent of the population. Of the nation's 65.8 million families, 6.9 million families, or 10.4 percent, lived in poverty.[5] Profiles of this poverty population follow a final word about the poverty thresholds.

15

CRITICS ATTACK CURRENT DEFINITION
OF POVERTY

Some of the debate that continues on the measurement of poverty focuses on the threshold approach that is now used. Some claim that the food plan used is out of date and would not, if it were used over a long period of time, be nutritionally satisfactory. Some criticize the "food times three" formula as unrealistic at a time when many poor families must spend well over 50 percent of their income on housing. (The multiplier used in 1988 was actually 3.3.) Other critics point out that variations in living costs in different regions of the country are not built into the thresholds.

Some reject the absolute approach to defining poverty. They suggest instead the use of a *relative* standard, focused on the distribution of income. They argue that poverty is more than just not having enough to get by, but a matter of having a lot less than others.

To illustrate how a relative standard of poverty would be used, assume that 50 percent of the national median income for a given family size is adopted as the poverty standard for families of that size. (This percentage is favored by some advocates of the relative approach.) In 1988 the median income of families of four was $39,051.[6] This means that half the four-person families had incomes below that figure and half had incomes above it. Under the 50-percent-of-median definition of poverty, the poverty standard for a family of four would have been over $19,000. Clearly, poverty standards tied to median incomes would send poverty rates soaring.

CHARACTERISTICS OF THE POOR
AS INDIVIDUALS[7]

The data that follow will support some widely held assumptions about the poor and challenge some others. Take, for example, the matter of poverty and race, as shown below.

Poverty Rates for Persons Grouped by Race and Hispanic Origin*

Number in the category (millions)		Below poverty level	
		%	Number (millions)
205.2	White	10.1	20.8
29.8	Black	31.6	9.4
8.5	Other races	20.0	1.7
20.1	Hispanic origin*	26.8	5.4
243.5	All persons	13.1	31.9

*Persons of Hispanic origin may be of any race. The vast majority of Hispanics, over 90 percent, are included in the white racial category in the Census Bureau's data. This is true even when a separate bar, as in this graphic, gives poverty data for all Hispanics, regardless of race. This footnote applies to all the graphs in the chapter.

A careless glance at the percentage bars would support the assumption that blacks outnumber whites in the poverty population. Actually, whites outnumber blacks by better than two to one. The explanation lies, of course, in the racial breakdown of the total population: 9.4 million poor blacks placed against a total black population of only 29.8 million produces a poverty percentage of 31.6 percent; 20.8 million white poor are only 10.1 percent of the total white population of 205.2 million, but the white poor constitute 65.1 percent of the 31.9 million poverty population. Thus, the racial distribution of the total poverty population in 1988 is depicted in the pie graph on the following page.

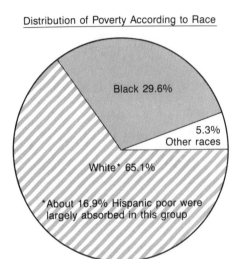

Distribution of Poverty According to Race

Black 29.6%

5.3%
Other races

White* 65.1%

*About 16.9% Hispanic poor were
largely absorbed in this group

Many associate poverty with the elderly but the graph below reveals just the opposite.

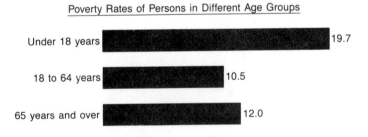

Poverty Rates of Persons in Different Age Groups

Under 18 years	19.7
18 to 64 years	10.5
65 years and over	12.0

In fact, a more detailed picture of poverty rates among the children and young people who make up the under-18 population group is troubling (see top of next page).

18

Racial Breakdown of the Under-18 Population

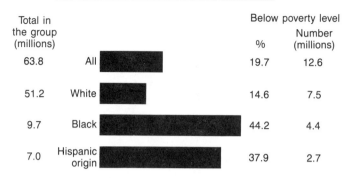

Total in the group (millions)			Below poverty level	
			%	Number (millions)
63.8	All		19.7	12.6
51.2	White		14.6	7.5
9.7	Black		44.2	4.4
7.0	Hispanic origin		37.9	2.7

A television or motion picture sequence involving poverty is very likely to be placed in an inner-city setting. But as the graphs below demonstrate, poverty exists in rural areas, suburban areas, small towns, big cities—in all kinds of places and all over the country.

Poverty Rates of Persons Who Live in Areas of Varied Population Density

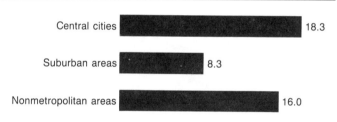

Central cities	18.3
Suburban areas	8.3
Nonmetropolitan areas	16.0

Poverty Rates of Persons Who Live in Different Areas of the Country

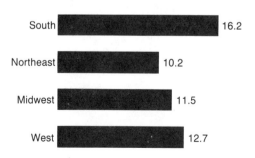

South	16.2
Northeast	10.2
Midwest	11.5
West	12.7

19

CHARACTERISTICS OF POOR FAMILIES

Turning from poverty data about individuals to data about families, one notices first that the poverty rate for families, 10.4 percent, is somewhat lower than the 13.1 percent rate for the total population. But within the broad category of families, the variations in poverty rates are extremely significant.

When families are grouped by race, this poverty pattern emerges.

Poverty Rates for Families Grouped by Race and Hispanic Origin

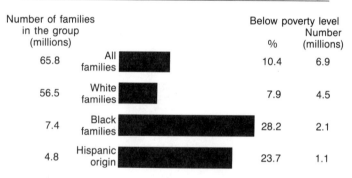

Number of families in the group (millions)		Below poverty level	
		%	Number (millions)
65.8	All families	10.4	6.9
56.5	White families	7.9	4.5
7.4	Black families	28.2	2.1
4.8	Hispanic origin	23.7	1.1

When families are grouped according to the level of education attained by the so-called householder (the head of the family), the poverty statistics send a clear message: income rises with education level.

Poverty Rates in Families Whose Householders' Education Level Varied

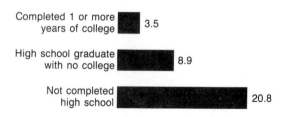

Completed 1 or more years of college — 3.5

High school graduate with no college — 8.9

Not completed high school — 20.8

The assumption that poverty is related to family size is supported by the following data:

Poverty Rates and Family Size

Number of families of that size (millions)			Families of that size below poverty level	
			%	Number (millions)
27.4	Two persons		8.5	2.3
15.4	Three persons		10.4	1.6
14.1	Four persons		9.9	1.4
6.1	Five persons		14.0	.9
1.9	Six persons		20.8	.4
.9	Seven or more		32.3	.3

The poverty rates of families with different employment histories in 1988 are troubling, but not surprising.

Poverty Rates of Families Grouped by 1988 Employment History

Number of families in the category (millions)			Below poverty level	
			%	Number (millions)
65.8	All families		10.4	6.9
38.5	Householder worked full time, year-round		2.9	1.1
9.7	Householder worked 49 weeks or fewer		19.4	1.9
14.7	Householder did not work		23.9	3.5

21

The final family data graph, below, highlights an aspect of the poverty problem that is viewed with rising concern.

Poverty Rates in Various Types of Families

Number of families in the category (millions)		Below poverty level	
		%	Number (millions)
65.8	All families	10.4	6.9
52.1	Married couples	5.8	2.9
7.4	Female householder with children, no spouse present	44.7	3.3
3.5	Female householder with no children, no spouse present	9.9	.3
2.8	Male householder, no spouse present	11.8	.3

It is easy to figure out what vexing problem those numbers highlight. There were 6.9 million poor families in the United States in 1988. Of those 6.9 million families, 3.6 million were families maintained by a female householder, with no spouse present. In other words, 53 percent of the poor families in the nation were headed by females with no spouse present; of the 2.1 million black families who live in poverty, an astonishing 75.6 percent were headed by females.

It is tempting to draw conclusions about poverty from data such as that presented in the preceding pages. One poverty expert, for example, made this observation:

The statistical profile of the poor shows quite clearly that those who manage to perform three quite elementary acts are very seldom counted among the persistently poor:
* *complete high school*
* *once an adult, get married and stay married (even if not on the first try)*

22

*· stay employed, even if at a wage and under
conditions below one's ultimate aim*[8]

A FIRST LOOK AT THE CAUSES OF POVERTY

The quotation above is an interesting prescription for avoiding poverty, but it sheds little light on the reasons why everybody does not achieve a stable, income-earning life. Why does poverty persist? Basically, it is because of the reality discussed early in this chapter. Inequality in the distribution of money income causes poverty. This incontrovertible statement obviously requires a follow-up. Why do some receive so little income and some so much? The answer depends upon whom you ask.

Probably the basic disagreement on causes of income inequality is between those who emphasize flaws in the economic system and those who emphasize flaws in those who are poor. Thus many liberals, those on the political left, assert that the nation's economic system does not always create enough jobs, or the right mix of jobs, so that all able-bodied individuals who want to work can find jobs at which they earn enough to provide adequately for those dependent upon them.

On the other hand, many conservatives, those on the political right, tend to stress the disabilities that keep poor people from lifting themselves out of their poverty: low aspirations, low motivation, weak commitment to a conviction that one *should* work. They point to behaviors that make upward mobility impossible: dropping out of school, poor job performance, early parenthood, alcohol and drug abuse. They point out the obvious barrier created by lack of skills. Emphasizing the persistence of poverty despite more than twenty years of a war on poverty, some go so far as to argue that the very programs designed to reduce poverty have operated to perpetuate it.

As the next chapter sharpens the picture of the poverty population by examining its two extremes, these causes will be seen at work.

23

In the land of opportunity, poverty exists in pockets everywhere. (Clockwise from top left) *In Lansing, Michigan, Native American children of migrant workers go without socks or shoes in winter. In an Appalachian mountain labor camp in North Carolina, a wood-burning stove heats the cabin that this white southern migrant family calls home. Migrant farm workers help themselves to soup, bread, and lemon pie in a soup kitchen funded by a local church in Immokalee, Florida. More than a dozen people live in a tiny apartment in Boston's Roxbury ghetto section.*

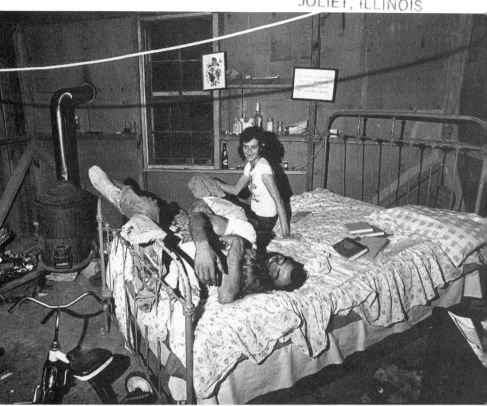

2
SHARPENING THE PICTURE OF THE POOR

"I sew front pockets," Filena Craft says of her work at the Reltoc Manufacturing Company . . . where she is among 100 workers who make men's cotton pants. Ms. Craft, who is 27 years old, earns the Federal minimum wage of $3.35 an hour and takes less than $100 a week home to the trailer where she lives with her two young daughters.[1]

Ms. Craft's income is below the poverty threshold for a family of three. She is one of the working poor.

THE WORKING POOR

If you are willing to work you can make it in this country. Most Americans really believe that. But if "making it" means escaping poverty, it's just not so. That's why the working poor are sometimes referred to as "America's glaring contradiction." Ask the 2.8 million people who worked 50 to 52 weeks in 1988 and earned incomes below the poverty level. Ask the 1.9 million of those 2.8 million who worked *full time* for 50 to 52 weeks and still ended up poor. (The standard definition of full-year full-time work is 35 hours per week for 50 weeks.)[2]

WHO ARE THE WORKING POOR?
The working poor are only a small fraction of the nation's fully employed labor force. About 79.6 million people worked full-time year-round in the United States in 1988 and only 2.4 percent of them, 1.9 million people, were poor. The vast majority of the working poor are white; two-thirds are men. (The female working poor make up the majority of the partially employed.) More than half live outside big cities.

Poor people in general nag at the conscience of this rich nation. But the 2.8 million people who worked year-round and ended up in poverty are especially disturbing. We feel indignant that people who work all year should be poor. They are doing the best they can.

WHAT ARE THE SPECIAL PROBLEMS
OF THE WORKING POOR?
Only 1.9 million of the 2.8 million poor who worked all year had full-time jobs. From many studies of part-time workers it is reasonable to assume that a substantial percentage of those who worked less than full time would have preferred a full schedule to their part-time status. The same is undoubtedly true of thousands who worked 49 or fewer weeks of the year.[3]

In other words, involuntary part-time work is a vexing problem for many of the working poor. Not only do many want more work, they want better jobs but lack either the basic education or the skills training to qualify for those better jobs.

The fortunes of the working poor vary directly with the health of the economy. "The rising tide" does not, despite the cliché, "lift all the boats." But a rising tide of prosperity does raise the fortunes and increase the working hours of the working poor. Conversely, hard times hit these vulnerable workers harder than others farther up the economic ladder.

The working poor derive far less benefit than the non-working poor from the social welfare programs that will be described in chapters 3 through 6. Training programs created to serve the hard-core unemployed are not open to them. Sometimes their wages are just fractionally too high for them to qualify for benefits, or sometimes their assets disqualify them. Ownership of a reasonably new car, for example, might make a person's financial picture look too rosy for food, housing, or medical care assistance. Probably more important, many of the working poor do not apply for public assistance benefits. They want no part of the welfare system.

Thus one of the acute needs of the working poor is health insurance. Many work for companies that offer no health insurance. Some who hold minimum wage jobs in companies that do offer optional health plans cannot afford the payroll deduction that would result from enrollment in the plan. Even companies with good health plans typically do not offer participation to their part-timers. Thus, millions of working poor are included among the 31 to 37 million Americans who, it is estimated, have no health insurance coverage.

Advocates of universal health insurance coverage offer varied proposals to solve this problem. Some urge requiring all employers to offer health insurance plans. Others claim that some form of national health insurance will have to be developed. All poverty experts urge that current eligibility rules for free or low-cost medical care be eased to admit the working poor to coverage.

WOULD A HIGHER MINIMUM WAGE HELP?

A traditional prescription for the plight of the working poor has been to raise the minimum wage. Ms. Craft, the young

Migrant laborers are among the millions of working poor that have no health insurance.

mother who sews front pockets, had her picture on the front page of a major newspaper because, after a political battle between President George Bush and Congress had gone on for months, such a raise was about to go into effect: from $3.35 to $3.80 per hour on April 1, 1990 with a second raise to $4.25 to take effect in April 1991. That adds up to slightly better than a 25 percent wage increase for the nation's approximately 3.2 million minimum-wage workers.[4]

Ironically, the newspaper story about the wage increase was headlined: "Rise in Minimum Wage Offers Minimum Joy." Ms. Craft and the other two workers whose reactions were reported are all single mothers with young children. Without knowing anything about poverty thresholds, they knew from their day-to-day struggle to get by that they would still be poor. A full-time worker on the minimum wage does not earn enough to exceed the poverty level for a family of three.

One young mother worried about the effect the raise would have on her food stamp allotment. (It would go down, for reasons explained in Chapter 4.) Another voiced the fear that the amount of output expected of workers would be increased, a legitimate worry since employers may recoup their higher wage costs by raising their output or their prices.

Experts disagree on the usefulness of raising the minimum wage as a poverty-reduction strategy. While some maintain that it can be an important part of such a strategy, others point out that the largest group of beneficiaries from such an increase is not the working poor but part-time workers from middle-income families in which there are other earners.

The argument is also made that if producers compensate for higher wage costs by raising prices, the benefits from the increased wage can easily be wiped out.

31

HOW MUCH DO TAX CREDITS
FOR CHILD CARE HELP?

The federal income tax code now permits working parents of children under four years old to deduct on their tax returns the costs they incur for child care. Some urge that permitting more liberal child care deductions would help the working poor, but the facts indicate otherwise. Permitting these deductions costs the government about $4 billion in forfeited taxes. But three-quarters of that amount was deducted by the wealthiest half of tax-paying families. Only about 3 percent of the $4 billion was deducted from the returns of the poorest 30 percent of families.[5]

ONE PROGRAM THAT
EVERYONE APPLAUDS: EITC

Starting without fanfare back in the 1970s, a change in the income tax law created a way to get additional cash income into the hands of working poor families with children without involving them in the social welfare system. Individuals and childless couples are ineligible to take advantage of the tax change. The provision is generally referred to as the Earned Income Tax Credit (EITC) but the Internal Revenue Service calls it the Earned Income Credit (EIC), a better name because one does not have to owe any income tax to take advantage of the credit. Here is how it works.

Richard Roe is married and has two children. In 1989 he earned $7,000, a poverty-level wage. He knew that on the basis of his income he was not required to file an income tax return but he also knew that he could get an earned income credit from the Internal Revenue Service if he filed a return claiming it. The credit is 14 percent of the first $6,500 of earnings; in other words, the maximum credit anyone can claim is $910. On the basis of Mr. Roe's $7,000 wage he was entitled to that maximum credit. He claimed it, and received a check for $910.

A worker who earns $2,300 can get an EIC of $324; an income of $5,000 would entitle a worker to a credit of $702. All workers who earn between $6,500 and $10,250 are entitled to claim the maximum credit of $910. At the wage level of $10,250 the credit begins to go down until incomes above $19,340 get no credit at all.

The rising credit at the lower end of the wage scale makes sense; there is no incentive to work less and collect a higher credit. The falling credit at the high end of the scale also makes sense; when your earnings approach $20,000, you don't need as much of a boost.

At the income levels where workers may owe some income tax, they simply subtract the tax they owe from their allowable credits and claim the difference.

EITC is becoming an important cash transfer program. In 1988 earned income credits totaling $4.9 billion were paid to 9.2 million families with children. In 1989 about 12.1 million families with children were expected to earn credits of $6.7 billion.[6]

There is almost universal support for EITC among poverty experts and among liberal and conservative political leaders. It is rightly viewed as a reward to those who work even though their efforts produce only modest earnings. The only objection raised to it is that there is no differentiation in the credit for families of different sizes. One suggestion for making such differentiation is to add 4 percent to the credit for each dependent child beyond one. Thus a family with three children would receive a credit of 26 percent.[7] Others have suggested making the credit more generous. For example, under a plan recently proposed by two members of the House of Representatives, a poor family with two preschool children could claim a 35 percent credit, up to a maximum of $2,450.[8]

The working poor and the deserving poor are synonymous terms in the public mind. Thus it is generally believed that the inequities that make their lives more difficult should be corrected. The program that reduces their poverty directly and efficiently should be strengthened. In short, we know what to do about the working poor. All we have to do is do it.

Unfortunately, no such consensus prevails about a second component of the poverty population.

THE UNDERCLASS

Is there an underclass? Here, says one journalist, are its voices.

> *He made me scared, so I pulled the trigger. So feel sorry? [sic] I doubt it. I didn't want to see him go down like that, but better him than me.*
> * * *
> *I'm gonna work 40 hours a week and bring home maybe $100, $150, when I can work 15 minutes and come back with $1,000 tax-free?*
> * * *
> *I ain't working for no minimum wage.*
> * * *
> *Man, you go two, three years not working, and hanging around and smoking reefer or drinking, and then you get a job—you can't handle it. You say, "I don't want to get up in the morning, get pushed and shoved. I'm gonna get on welfare."*
> * * *
> *Everybody else I knew was having babies, so I just went along.*
> * * *
> *It just seems that everybody here is down on their luck.*[9]

And these, he asserts, are the people of whom these attitudes are typical.

> *Who are the underclass? They are poor; but numbering around five million, they are a rela-*

34

tively small minority of the 33 million Ameri-
cans with incomes below the official poverty line.
Disproportionately black and Hispanic, they are
still a minority within these minorities. What
primarily defines them is not so much their pov-
erty or race as their behavior—their chronic
lawlessness, drug use, out-of-wedlock births,
nonwork, welfare dependency, and school fail-
ure. "Underclass" describes a state of mind and
a way of life. It is at least as much a cultural
as an economic condition.[10]

A CONTROVERSIAL TERM

Many who deplore the use of the term *underclass* and the
frequently associated term, *culture of poverty,* would find
the last sentence of that definition objectionable. Such terms
and statements, they argue, suggest that innate character-
istics peculiar to the members of the problem population
explain their lack of progress. To talk of a culture of poverty, the argument continues, is to deny the unique historic
burden that slavery and its aftermath placed upon the majority group among that so-called "problem population,"
blacks. It is blaming victims for the condition to which
society has reduced them.

It would appear, however, that use of the term underclass has gained increasing acceptance. Perhaps this definition by William Julius Wilson, a distinguished black sociologist, has helped to foster that acceptance.

Today's ghetto neighborhoods are populated al-
most exclusively by the most disadvantaged seg-
ments of the black urban community, that het-
erogeneous grouping of families and individuals
who are outside the mainstream of the Ameri-
can economic system. Included in this group are
individuals who lack training and skills and either
experience long-term unemployment or are not

members of the labor force, individuals who are engaged in street crime and other forms of aberrant behavior, and families that experience long-term spells of poverty and/or welfare dependency. These are the populations to which I refer when I speak of the underclass.[11]

Notice that this definition, like that of the journalist, specifically includes race as a distinguishing underclass characteristic but focuses on blacks, as do most who address the problem. Unlike the journalist's definition, it puts the underclass in a specific setting, the urban ghettos.

Some who treat the subject of the underclass make a point of calling attention to a white underclass, a rural underclass. But others point out that only blacks have been confined by segregationist practices to specific areas, the ghettos. There, they argue, because blacks are physically

Isolated from the American economic mainstream, the most disadvantaged poor—so-called the underclass—*have emerged out of the urban ghettoes.* (Top) *Teenage boys shoot the breeze in a poor Brooklyn neighborhood, where garbage cans are a common part of the landscape.* (Bottom) *As residents of one of Boston's tenements, children are exposed to disease every day as they live and play in filthy living quarters.*

isolated from mainstream life, a tangle of problems—unemployment, crime, addiction, out-of-wedlock births, welfare dependency—has become the ghetto way of life.

This is a new view of the ghetto, which is one reason the sociologist quoted above argues for use of *underclass* to describe the problem people who live there. The new term, he maintains, emphasizes the reality that today's ghetto population is a new phenomenon, unique in United States social history. The background of that phenomenon, he explains, lies in the post-World War II experience of the urban black population.

THE EMERGENCE OF TODAY'S GHETTOS

In the post-war years a massive migration of blacks from the South into the cities of the North brought a new population to the urban ghettos, just as waves of migration from other countries had brought other thousands to those ghettos in earlier years. As the earlier newcomers from abroad settled into their new country and started moving up the economic ladder, they moved out of the ghettos, but this moving-on phase of the immigrant experience was closed to blacks. Racial segregation kept them in the limited urban areas that had been open to them; many urban ghettos became virtually black ghettos.

All blacks were confined, but many did well on the economic ladder. Thus the black urban communities contained people who had achieved a wide range of success. Black workers brought home good wages from secure blue collar jobs. Black middle-class professionals lived in different neighborhoods of the ghetto from working-class blacks but mingled routinely with them. Black doctors served black patients, black ministers headed the churches, children from all kinds of homes mingled in the schools. Mainstream patterns of behavior, visibly present in the community, fostered stability. Then came the civil rights movement of the 1960s.

Nobody claims that the civil rights movement has ended segregation. In fact a 1989 report on black progress asserts that "full integration of blacks into a color-blind society is unlikely in any foreseeable future."[12] However, while housing barriers distressingly persist, many successful professionals and some working-class blacks have left the ghettos.

WIDENING RIFTS AMONG BLACKS

The differences between blacks in the ghetto and blacks who have moved into mainstream American life are sharp. Income disparity between blacks and whites continues to be disturbing, but the gap between incomes of black and white *married-couple families* has narrowed significantly.

Median family income 1988[13]

	White	Black
All families	$33,915	$19,319
Married-couple families	36,840	30,385

Black families outside the ghetto are overwhelmingly married-couple families. The low-income black families who pull the "all-black families" median down are in the ghetto.

Left behind in the ghettos are thousands of black unmarried women and their children, many born out of wedlock. Opportunities for women of today's ghettos to marry are disproportionately low. The worsening job situation for black men partially explains one estimate that for every 100 black women there are only 45 employed, civilian black men.[14] Other causes that contribute to that ratio are the high rate of deaths from violence among young black ghetto men, their high rate of imprisonment, and their high drop-out rate from the labor market.

Left behind are the street criminals, the drug dealers, the children who take their disadvantaged backgrounds to school, the mothers who try to do a good job of raising their families alone, and the mothers who have ceased to nurture their young because crack has destroyed them.

Where are the people of the underclass in the poverty data of Chapter 1? Some are certainly among those poor families whose householder had not completed high school; some are among the 3.5 million poor families whose householder did not work in 1988; troubling numbers are certainly among the 3.6 million poor female-headed families.

INTRODUCING THE PUBLIC WELFARE SYSTEM

The picture that has been drawn of the extremes in the poverty population suggests some of the reasons why there is a public welfare system. Entering that system is not easy or pleasant. In fact, as one reads about the bureaucratic procedures applicants must follow in various programs it is mind-boggling that people of limited education can work their way through the maze.

Many applicants find it difficult to retain their dignity and self-respect as they wait, and wait, and wait, sometimes in squalid welfare offices for interviews with social workers who may be courteous, compassionate, and helpful or callously rude and indifferent.

It's not easy to tell everything there is to be known about every member of their households, report everything about their income and assets, describe details about their way of life such as, perhaps, how they buy and prepare food. And then, having coped with that office, they find that the other assistance they seek requires more information, in another form.

A social worker employed by the Chinatown Planning Association assists an applicant.

On the other hand, the picture that has been drawn of the extremes suggests the wide range of problems that policy makers confront in the effort to reduce poverty. The chapters that follow describe programs that have been devised to that end. As you read about these programs, bear in mind that every detail in every program is a response to a demonstrated need. Legislators do not dream up poverty programs in a vacuum. In the hearings that precede any major piece of legislation, people report their needs in very human terms; professionals report their experiences among the target populations; administrators warn of safeguards that must be built into helping programs to ensure that they will help the right people rather than the unscrupulous.

The nation has not always done its best, but as of now, here is what we do about poverty.

3
INCOME MAINTENANCE PROGRAMS

What would be the simplest and most direct way to end poverty in the United States? No problem. Give poor people enough money to lift them out of poverty. No legislator has ever proposed a program that would go that far, but poor people in the United States do receive cash income from the federal government under a variety of income maintenance programs. The government, in other words, redistributes income.

Middle- and upper-income (even some low-income) individuals pay income taxes. The government gives some of the money raised by those taxes to individuals and families who have very low incomes or no incomes at all. In the government's financial accounts these outlays are categorized as *transfer payments,* a term that means expenditures for which no service is rendered or product delivered. Cash payments in this category are called *cash transfers.* Needless to say, some people think far too much of this goes on, others think far too little.

In 1988* the federal government made cash transfers totaling about $32.2 billion to needy families or individuals. Those cash transfers were included in the $3.2 trillion aggregate income received by households in 1988. In spite of this $32.2 billion of cash public assistance we have seen that 13.1 percent of the people of the United States were poor in 1988, but without those transfers the poverty rate would have been significantly higher.[1] For example, in 1985, when the official poverty rate was 14.0 percent, experts estimate that without cash public assistance the rate would have been 14.9.[2]

AID TO FAMILIES WITH DEPENDENT CHILDREN

The federal public welfare system comprises more than seventy federal programs that offer cash and noncash need-based benefits.[3] But in the public mind, a family "on welfare" is a family receiving money from AFDC, the Aid to Families with Dependent Children program. This is a so-called *income maintenance* program and it is by far the largest and most controversial of all the public assistance programs in that category.

HOW AFDC WORKS

AFDC is a joint federal/state program on which the federal government spent $10.3 billion in 1988 to serve an AFDC population of 10.9 million persons. The states spent an

---

*The Census Bureau's year is the calendar year but the federal government's financial records are kept in fiscal years. So in this and subsequent chapters 1988 means October 1, 1987, through September 30, 1988. Thus poverty data for 1988 and government expenditures to reduce poverty are three months out of sync, but for the purposes of this book the two kinds of years can be used together without distorting the conclusions drawn.

additional $8.7 billion.[4] Federal legislation establishes basic ground rules for AFDC, but each state sets its own eligibility rules and level of benefits.

When the program was initiated in 1935 as part of the Social Security Act, the original name, Aid to Dependent Children, made clear that children are the target group. Adults receive the AFDC checks, but only because they are the care-givers for children. Childless families, however needy, are ineligible for AFDC. When the youngest child in an AFDC family reaches age eighteen, aid stops. Under the original intent of the program, children were to be deemed needy who lived with one parent because the other parent was either dead or not living in the child's home. Children living with two parents were "needy" only if one parent was unable to work. Under these provisions, widows were for years the chief beneficiaries of the program.

In the 1960s the AFDC rolls were opened to two-parent families if the family wage earner was unemployed. States were authorized to offer AFDC-UP (Unemployed Parent) programs. So there are some two-parent AFDC families, namely families headed by disabled or unemployed fathers.

But in 1988, 90 percent of AFDC households were headed by divorced, separated, abandoned, or never-married mothers. These mothers, along with the widows for whom AFDC was originally created, make up the category in the census data: "female householder, no spouse present." Has the percentage of such families increased over the years? Of all the families with children under age eighteen, one out of thirty-three was receiving AFDC aid in 1960; in 1988 the ratio was almost one in eight.[5]

SOME MISCONCEPTIONS
Long-term welfare dependents mired in the underclass are unquestionably a serious problem but all kinds of miscon-

ceptions cloud the public's image of the AFDC population as a whole. Some of them are:

"Lots of families on welfare are better off than families supported by a full-time year-round worker." Actually it is impossible to generalize about the way of life that AFDC makes possible, because the benefits vary greatly from state to state. For example, as of January 1989 the monthly benefit for a family of three was $118 in Alabama, $663 in California, and $809 in Alaska.[6]

Overall, AFDC benefits reduce the hardships associated with poverty but do little to reduce the poverty rate. For while it is true that in eight states the 1986 benefit level for a family of four was higher than the income from full-time work at the minimum wage, the average monthly cash benefit for one-parent–two-children families, as of December 1988, was $367, well below the poverty level.[7]

"They stay on the rolls year after year after year." The truth is that about half of those who enter AFDC receive benefits for two years or fewer.[8] In other words, for many, AFDC is the needed lifeline in a time of crisis such as job loss, divorce, death or disablement of the principal wage earner in a previously intact family.

It is also true, however, that about one-quarter of those who enter the program receive aid for nine years or more.[9] And since their years of participation overlap, at any given time long-term welfare dependents constitute about 60 percent of the AFDC caseload.[10] These are the problem cases that, by the late 1980s, created the demand for welfare reform.

"There wouldn't be so many unmarried teenage mothers if welfare benefits weren't available." Despite the frequency with which this assertion is made, the consensus among poverty experts seems to be that there is little convincing supporting evidence for it. On the other hand, research does seem to support the claim that the availability of benefits encourages young, single mothers to live independently rather than in their parents' households.

WORK AND WELFARE

Social welfare researchers repeatedly study the effect of cash transfer programs on recipients' work effort. A typical research problem might be: How did Program X affect the number of hours worked by people in the program?

This is a matter of concern for two reasons. Americans do not like programs that increase dependence, that decrease recipients' feeling of responsibility for taking care of themselves and their families. Second, anything that reduces the amount of labor that goes into producing goods and services reduces the size of the nation's economic pie and, in the long run, the prosperity of all of us depends upon the size of that pie.

Repeated studies of the work history of AFDC recipients have established that the percentage of AFDC mothers who work is consistently low, never higher than 18 percent.[11] Since the program was originally devised to ensure that women with young children could stay home and take care of them, the low rate of participation in the labor market was, for many years, not considered troublesome.

That attitude has changed as increasing numbers of nonpoor women have gone out to work. Thus in recent years a number of federal employment and training programs (described in Chapter 6) have included AFDC mothers, and a few states have built into their AFDC programs a *workfare* requirement for mothers of school-age children. Workfare operates like this: Assume that Jenny, a welfare mother, receives a monthly benefit of $380. Her social worker divides that figure by the hourly minimum wage of $3.80, and tells Jenny that she must work 100 hours each month at the public service job in which she is to be placed to "work off" her benefit. Jenny receives no other remuneration for her work. It's work for welfare.

Critics of workfare point out that it can produce situations like this: Jenny, the welfare mother, is seated next to Carrie, a minimum-wage worker, in the government office to which she is assigned. Carrie knows that Jenny is getting the same rate of pay that she is. Carrie also knows that because Jenny is on AFDC she is eligible for free medical care. Carrie can't afford to buy the optional medical insurance available in her office. Is this fair?

Regardless of the problems that arise when states try to get women off welfare and into jobs, the attempt goes on. Where the pressure in that direction finally led will be seen when the Family Support Act of 1988 is analyzed.

OTHER INCOME MAINTENANCE AND CASH BENEFIT PROGRAMS

The programs listed in Figure 3-1 suggest the wide range of poor people's problems for which cash transfer programs have been developed.

The most important of these cash benefit programs are described below.

SUPPLEMENTAL SECURITY INCOME

With 1988 federal expenditures of $11.7 billion and state expenditures of about $3 billion, Supplemental Security Income (SSI) ranks second in importance among the federal government's income maintenance programs.[12]

It is a much less controversial program than AFDC because it serves people generally considered deserving. As of 1989 the SSI population consisted of about 1.4 million needy aged, about 83,000 blind, and almost 3 million disabled.[13]

SSI is primarily a federal program, but states that had, before SSI, cash benefit programs for the needy aged, blind, and disabled continue to make payments under those programs that supplement the federal income grants.

SSI benefits, while modest, are more generous than those under AFDC. The minimum monthly benefit in 1989 was $368.[14] More important, benefits are adjusted annually as the cost of living rises. Thus, while a substantial majority of SSI individuals and a significant percentage of

Figure 3-1. Cash Benefits to the Poor

	Federal expenditures (millions of current dollars) FY1988	Recipients (average monthly number unless otherwise indicated— in thousands) FY1988
Aid to Families with Dependent Children (AFDC)	$10,302	10,920
Supplemental Security Income (SSI)	11,663	4,302
Earned Income Tax Credit (EITC)	4,927	27,741
Pensions for Needy Veterans, Their Dependents, and Survivors	3,862	1,201
General Assistance (nonmedical care component)	0	1,145
Foster Care	888	123
Adoption Assistance	114	33.0
Emergency Assistance	96.2	134
Assistance to Refugees and Cuban/Haitian Entrants (cash component)	163	76
Dependency and Indemnity Compensation and Death Compensation for Parents of Veterans	101	55
General Assistance to Indians	67.5	69.1
Cash aid total	$32,181	

Source: U.S. Library of Congress, Congressional Research Service, CRS Report for Congress No. 89-595 EPW, Cash and Noncash Benefits for Persons with Limited Income: Eligibility Rules, Recipient and Expenditure Data, FY 1986–88, October 24, 1989, p. 210.

SSI couples remain poor, the program lifts higher percentages out of poverty than does AFDC.

The major weakness of the program appears to be that many whom it could serve are not being served, although its administrators have tried to locate and enroll the estimated two million people who are eligible and not receiving benefits. Some who know they qualify do not apply

49

for SSI because they would feel stigmatized if they were part of a welfare program. Other thousands of eligible nonparticipants do not know about the program or, being vaguely aware of it, fail to realize how substantially it could help them.

Gwendolyn S. King, commissioner of Social Security, is determined to get the SSI message out to people whose lives could be changed by that message. As she told a reporter,

> . . . *she had sought to set an example by putting on blue jeans, a sweater and ski jacket and accompanying agency field workers as they approached homeless men and women in Baltimore, the headquarters of the Social Security Administration, which administers the S.S.I. program.* She recognizes that getting the word out will not be easy, adding: *"We had several people promise to come into the shelter that night, where people were going to take applications. . . . Some people came and some did not."* [15]

VETERANS' PENSIONS

The Veterans' Pension program probably enjoys the broadest popular acceptance. So widely held is the idea that veterans of wartime military service are deserving that many do not think of the program as welfare. Nonetheless it is a public assistance program in that eligibility (with one exception) and benefits are based on financial need rather than prior earnings.

Eligible for benefits under the program are low-income wartime veterans (the wartime service need be only one day) over 65, permanently and totally disabled wartime veterans, and survivors of wartime veterans. Neither the disability nor death need be service related. Veterans disabled during military service are eligible for disability compensation payments. For these, no income, or need, test is required.

GENERAL ASSISTANCE AND
EMERGENCY ASSISTANCE

Broad as is the coverage of the federal and federal/state programs thus far described, there remain a sizable number of poor people who need public assistance. Some have been accepted for programs but are waiting for benefits to reach them; some are childless couples and singles ineligible for AFDC; some were on AFDC but lost eligibility when their youngest child reached age eighteen; some may be partially disabled or vision impaired but not to a degree that meets SSI requirements. Then there is that growing cohort of the needy—the homeless. Whatever help these people receive is dispensed under state and local programs that are usually called General Assistance.

No federal funds are provided for General Assistance, but 50 percent federal funding is provided for a program called Emergency Assistance, which serves needy families with children, including migrant families. The Social Security Act, which authorizes the program, allows states to give cash and other forms of aid for no more than thirty days per year.

Each state program defines the kind of emergencies in which Emergency Assistance benefits will be paid. Most cover natural disasters and unspecified crises threatening family or living arrangements. Among the other emergencies listed in state programs are homelessness, eviction or threat of eviction or foreclosure on a mortgage, utility shutoff, health or safety hazards.

TWO SPECIAL PROGRAMS
FOR NEEDY CHILDREN

Welfare agencies must frequently place children from low-income families in foster care homes, at state expense. The Foster Care program, by supplying federal matching funds for this purpose, makes better foster care placements possible.

Hundreds of children awaiting adoption are difficult to place because they have "special needs." Some have mental or physical disabilities; some are outside the age range preferred by adopting families; some are difficult to match with adopting families because of race; some are in sibling groups that are being held together. Under the Adoption Assistance program, federal matching funds match the assistance payments that states offer as an inducement to adopting parents to take on a child with special needs.

SOCIAL SECURITY

Social insurance does more to prevent poverty in the United States than any of the *public assistance* cash transfer programs that have been discussed in this chapter. The nation's major social insurance program is Old Age and Survivors Insurance (OASI), which was introduced in the 1930s during the New Deal and now covers most of the nation's

In 1985 senior citizens gathered in Harrisburg, Pennsylvania, to celebrate the fiftieth anniversary of the Social Security program and to protest President Ronald Reagan's proposed cuts in Social Security benefits. The women hold up cakes that say "Cut the Cake, Not the C.O.L.A." [Cost of Living Allowance].

work force. When Disability Insurance (DI) was added in 1956, the program became OASDI. Medicare (to be discussed in Chapter 4) was added to the social insurance roster in 1965. Federally supported unemployment insurance dating back to the New Deal is also a social insurance program. Thus, social insurance is a very broad term. The term *Social Security,* however, as it is used in the federal government's budget documents and financial reports, refers to OASDI outlays only. And they are huge: $232.5 billion in 1989. Only "military" expenditures of $303.6 billion exceeded them; interest expenditures of $169.1 billion ranked third.[16]

The social insurance programs were not specifically designed to reduce poverty but rather to insure workers—and their dependents and survivors—against the earnings losses associated with retirement, death, disability, or temporary unemployment. Nonetheless, the degree to which they prevent poverty is substantial. For example, about 47 percent of Social Security dollars go to persons who would be "poor," in terms of poverty thresholds, if they were not receiving Social Security benefits.[17]

DESCRIPTION OF THE PROGRAM
In the public mind people "on Social Security" are retired persons who receive, or have credited to their bank accounts, Social Security benefits. This is the way OASI, the program under which those benefits are issued, works.

Social Security benefits are based on a person's work history. Fully insured participants must have worked at least ten years in jobs where their earnings were subject to the Social Security payroll tax, which also automatically assures their participation in the hospital insurance part of the Medicare program.

The payroll tax has been the source of considerable political controversy. While income taxes were being lowered during the 1980s, the Social Security payroll tax was rising. As of January 1, 1990, the rate deducted from workers' wages and matched by employers' contributions was 7.65 percent—6.2 percent for retirement benefits and 1.45 for the hospital insurance part of Medicare. As a result of the two tax trends, the share of federal revenues raised by income taxes fell by 6 percent during the 1980s while the share raised from Social Security taxes rose 23 percent.

The income tax is progressive, that is, the tax burden increases as income increases. In contrast, the Social Security payroll tax is regressive, that is, the tax burden decreases as income increases. Here's why: There is a ceiling on the amount of income subject to the Social Security payroll tax, a ceiling of $51,300 (as of this writing). Lower-income workers have the 7.65 percent payroll tax applied to the full amount of their wages, while workers earning high salaries have no payroll tax deducted from the portion of their salaries that exceeds $51,300.[18] Thus the tax paid by high-income workers is actually lower than 7.65 percent.

Critics deplore covering an increasing share of the costs of government by a regressive tax. They also point out that the huge sums currently flowing into the federal treasury from Social Security payroll taxes exceed the amount being paid out in Social Security benefits. This, critics maintain, conceals the real size of the federal budget deficit.

SOME BROADER QUESTIONS
ABOUT SOCIAL SECURITY

Social Security is, understandably, a very popular program. And because current benefits are linked to past earnings, beneficiaries entertain no doubts about deserving what they get. Furthermore, current workers whose taxes are paying for today's retirees bear no grudge about their burden. They are confident that tax receipts from tomorrow's workers will pay their benefits.

But the system has been challenged on some basic grounds. Some maintain that Social Security discourages saving, which reduces the funds available for investment and thus hampers economic growth. Others feel that growth toward a bigger economic pie is slowed by Social Security's effect on the labor supply, the inducement it offers to retire earlier than would be possible without its benefits. Research on these subjects has shown some impact on the labor supply but no conclusive evidence of a negative impact on savings.

Against these concerns, however, stands the Social Security record as the most effective poverty-reduction program in the United States. In the public mind, Social Security is an unqualified success.

4
IN-KIND TRANSFER PROGRAMS

Suppose ten people are asked: Do you consider unequal distribution of income a major problem in the United States? Those who know what the question means are very likely to answer no. But if ten people are asked: "Does it trouble you that there are children in the United States who go to bed hungry?," almost certainly the result will be ten affirmative answers.

CASH VERSUS IN-KIND BENEFITS

Many people who are unaware of, or indifferent to, the income disparity that makes people poor are touched by evidence of the hardships poverty can cause: hunger, substandard housing, and the absence of health care. They are willing to support programs that meet these specific needs. Many believe, furthermore, that while income maintenance checks may be spent unwisely, medical care benefits are bound to be applied to health problems, and food stamps are bound to relieve hunger.

Legislators are understandably sensitive to public attitudes on social welfare programs so it is not surprising that, as Figure 4-1 shows, seven of every ten federal dollars spent on social welfare programs go for noncash needs-tested programs. Figure 4-2 shows that medical care, food, and housing are the major benefit areas.[1] Noncash benefits are called *in-kind transfers* to distinguish them from the cash transfers described in the previous chapter.

Figure 4-1. Outlays for Means-Tested Assistance (1960–1986)

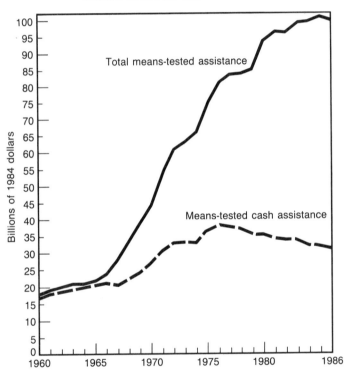

Source: Sheldon H. Danziger and Daniel H. Weinberg, eds.,
Fighting Poverty: What Works and What Doesn't (Cambridge, Mass.:
Harvard University Press, 1986), p.22

58

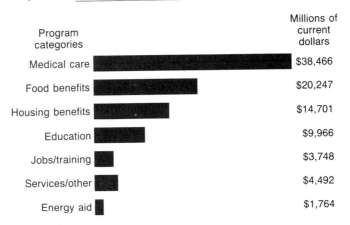

Figure 4-2. Federal Expenditures on Major Need-Tested Programs

Program categories		Millions of current dollars
Medical care		$38,466
Food benefits		$20,247
Housing benefits		$14,701
Education		$9,966
Jobs/training		$3,748
Services/other		$4,492
Energy aid		$1,764

Source: U.S. Library of Congress, Congressional Research Service, CRS Report for Congress No. 89-595 EPW, Cash and Noncash Benefits for Persons with Limited Income: Eligibility Rules, Recipient and Expenditure Data, FY 1986–88, October 24, 1989, p. 2.

Cash benefits received by poor households are counted by the Census Bureau in its income statistics. It does *not* count as income the value of the noncash benefits those households receive. Critics of that Census Bureau policy maintain that failure to count in-kind benefits as income makes the poverty rate appear worse than it really is.

In response to that criticism the Census Bureau does a separate series of calculations. It adds to households' reported cash income its calculation of certain noncash benefits the households report receiving. They include valuations of Medicaid coverage, food stamps, rent subsidies, and free and reduced-price school lunches. With incomes calculated on that basis, the poverty rate in 1988 would have been 10.5 percent. However, despite the fact that Census Bureau reports covering 1988 contain "in-kind benefits included" income and poverty data, the official rate, excluding in-kind benefits, remains 13.1 percent. That is the rate released to the press and generally cited.

It is worth noting that not all recipients of noncash

benefits share the public and legislative preference for that form of assistance. Using food stamps, living in public housing, are very open announcements of dependency; cashing a welfare check can be a much more private transaction.

MEDICAL BENEFITS

Medicaid is by far the nation's largest public assistance program. It is a joint federal/state venture, the federal government sharing the costs of the states' programs and mandating certain services that the states must provide in their programs.

Two groups are served by Medicaid. One (called the categorically needy) includes people who fall into categories presumed to need medical assistance: families or individuals who receive AFDC or SSI benefits, pregnant women who will become eligible for AFDC when their babies are born, needy pregnant women in two-parent families, and needy children up to age seven. All state programs must serve the categorically needy.

States are also reimbursed for medical benefits offered to individuals or families whose income is slightly too high to qualify for cash benefits but who are incurring such heavy medical bills that the income they have left is below the cash benefit standard. These people are called the medically needy.

Among the services that federal law requires the states to offer to the needy are hospital care, laboratory tests, care in a skilled nursing facility, some home care, and physicians' services. With some exceptions, notably in the interests of children and pregnant women, states may require Medicaid recipients to pay small fees as "copayments."

About two-thirds of the 23.9 million individuals served by Medicaid in 1988 were from AFDC households.[2] But medical care for the elderly and disabled is much more expensive than that for younger AFDC recipients. Nursing home care, for example, accounted for about four out of every ten dollars that Medicaid spent,[3] with the result that, overall, 70 percent of its over $30 billion outlays was for care of the elderly and disabled.[4]

The federal government maintains a wide variety of other medical benefit programs and the positive impact of these programs on the nation's health is almost universally acknowledged. Widely criticized, however, are three glaring weaknesses in the nation's health care picture. The poor are being helped, but not all doctors will serve them because they consider Medicaid's reimbursement levels too low. Medicaid patients must travel farther and wait longer for medical attention; they are unlikely to be referred to specialists. Second, there is a substantial variation among the states in the extent of Medicaid coverage and the range of services offered. Third is the glaring weakness noted in Chapter 2: the growing number of persons not poor enough for Medicaid, not old enough for Medicare, and unable to afford private health insurance plans.

FOOD BENEFITS

Food-for-the-poor programs began as far back as the 1930s, but those early distributions were not designed primarily to reduce poverty. They aimed to support food prices by keeping surpluses off the market. The shift to real food assistance began in the 1960s, and by the 1970s Congress had mandated that the present Food Stamp program be offered in all the states.

The Food Stamp program is the most federal of all the in-kind benefit programs; eligibility rules and benefit levels are uniform in all states. States administer the program but the federal government reimburses them for over half the costs of administration and for all the benefits— more than $13 billion in 1988.[5]

Second only to Medicaid in federal needs-tested spending, the Food Stamp program served over 20 million low-income persons each month of 1988.[6] Because families and individuals in the AFDC and SSI programs are automatically eligible for food stamps, households with children constitute over 60 percent of the program's beneficiaries; about 20 percent of food stamp households include elderly members, and at least 7 percent include disabled individuals. Other households that receive food stamps even though there is a working member qualify because of their low incomes.[7]

Food Stamp eligibility requirements offer an interesting example of the effort to keep social welfare legislation and regulations attuned to human needs: applicants cannot be denied food stamps simply because they are homeless. On the other side of the coin, the regulations also reflect the popular conviction that people should work for what they get. Unemployed, able-bodied adult recipients are supposed to prove that they are meeting specific job search requirements or that they are enrolled in a job training program.

The amount a family receives in food stamps is determined by a process that sounds complicated. But the complications stem from the effort to meet the enormous diversity of applicants' situations and needs. Here is an example of what happens.

Suppose a family of three had a monthly cash income of $800 in 1988. First the deductions from income allowed by the regulations are subtracted from that $800. This family paid a higher rent than is considered affordable on an $800 income so there was a deduction for that; the elderly family member required care while the others were at work so there was a deduction for that expense. The family ended up with a "counted income" of $274. The maximum monthly food stamp benefit for a family of three was set in 1988 at $236. That's how much it would have cost that year to feed a family of three the meals prescribed in the Economy Food Plan (the same plan that was used in computing the poverty thresholds). Now, says the social worker who is computing the benefit, you can afford to spend 30 percent of your "counted income" for food. That's $82.20. Since your family needs to spend $236 for an adequate diet, you will receive $153 worth of food stamps each month.

Once the food stamps are in hand, more regulations follow the recipients into the 200,000 establishments that are authorized to accept them. There they may buy "food for home preparation and human consumption, not including alcohol, tobacco, or hot foods intended for immediate consumption."[8] In the interests of the thousands of elderly whom the program serves, stamps may be used for "meals-on-wheels." Change of less than one dollar is given to food stamps purchasers in cash but the law specifically forbids a series of transactions deliberately engineered to yield enough cash to buy a forbidden product.

As long as stamp holders are buying food, they can buy balanced diets or nutritional nightmares and some critics of the program deplore the fact that it does nothing to improve the nutrition level of households served.

In contrast, the federal food programs that focus on children are structured to achieve nutritional goals. Almost all the young people in the United States attend schools that participate in the National School Lunch program, which is paid for with federal money plus matching local school district funds. Under this program, enrolled children from needy families receive free or reduced-price lunches. Each lunch menu must follow a federally prescribed meal pattern and must supply one-third of the child's required daily quota of vitamins and minerals.

Children not eligible for the free or reduced-price lunch can buy it at the so-called full price. The full price is still less than what the market price of the lunch would be, which prompts critics to point out that despite recent efforts to correct the situation some children from very prosperous families are eating at least partially subsidized school lunches. Supporters of the program, on the other hand,

Children attending kindergarten in New York participate in the National School Lunch program.

deplore the fact that some nonparticipating school districts remain outside the program not because they don't need it but because they can't afford it.

WIC (Special Supplemental Food Program for Women, Infants, and Children) is an attempt to ensure that needy women, before and after the birth of their babies, include in their diets foods likely to minimize the risks associated with low-birth-weight infants. (These women's children under age five are also included in the program.) The vouchers used in this program, unlike food stamps, can be used only for specific items such as fortified cereal, eggs, juice, milk, formula, and cheese.

Studies have found real gains in infant well-being from this program but the findings are not universally accepted. Supporters stress that later years will produce additional payoff from the nutritional boost received in childhood and deplore the fact that pressure on state budgets has resulted in cutbacks in food allotments for the program.[9]

HOUSING

Most of the in-kind benefit programs described thus far are targeted at reducing the effects of poverty. Federal housing legislation, while targeted to a degree on the needs of low-income homeseekers, pursues a wide range of other goals: smoothing out upswings and downturns in the housing construction industry; increasing home ownership by assistance to home buyers; assisting groups with special housing problems, such as minorities and the physically handicapped; stimulating employment; and revitalizing neighborhoods and urban areas.

Low-income families, mostly renters, have always had a hard time finding decent, affordable housing. Today the shortage of such housing has assumed crisis proportions. Thousands of housing units have disappeared from the housing market because owners have abandoned them, allowed them to be seized for nonpayment of taxes. Other thousands disappeared when urban renewal projects cleared slums without creating new housing to replace what had been destroyed.

Many low-income families, to avoid paying rents they cannot afford, settle for housing units in buildings that are substandard in construction and/or maintenance. When even low-quality housing is not available at affordable prices many poor households are forced to spend what they cannot afford, an unacceptably high percentage of their limited incomes. Many pay 50 percent of their incomes, or more, for shelter.

For some low-income individuals and families, federal programs have offered a solution to their housing problems. Public housing, despite its acknowledged shortcomings, offers the poor decent housing at rentals within their means. Billions were spent on the construction of public housing projects and, even with new construction virtually at a standstill, substantial federal outlays on public housing are required each year. The low rents permitted by federal law do not begin to cover the cost of maintaining project buildings, and an enormous backlog of needed repairs has accumulated over the years.

Federal housing programs of recent years have focused on making privately constructed housing available to low-income homeseekers at affordable rents. Under one program, builders received substantial financial assistance for the construction of multiple-unit housing in return for agreements that they would maintain rents at affordable levels.

Other programs have tried to make existing housing available to low-income renters. Some low-income households receive housing certificates or vouchers. These are promises made by the federal government to owners of rental housing units. They say, in effect: If you rent an apartment to the holder of this certificate or voucher, he or she will pay one-third of his income toward the rent you are charging. (Rents are regulated by the Department of

Housing and Urban Development.) We will pay you the balance.

Housing benefits are substantial and, if counted as income, would lift many of the poor households lucky enough to get them above the poverty level. The key word in that last sentence is "lucky." AFDC, SSI, and Medicaid are entitlement programs. Any individual or household that meets the eligibility standards and applies for the benefits receives them. But there is no such thing as a housing entitlement program. Public housing projects have long waiting lists; the low budget appropriations of recent years have meant sharply limited funds to subsidize rentals in private housing. Less than 30 percent of those eligible for rent assistance get it.[10]

Homeless people sleeping in the streets would seem a powerful incentive for government to do more about housing than is now being done. For whatever other problems burden the lives of the homeless, their *homelessness* is a housing problem. The private construction industry cannot, without government subsidies, build rental housing that can be offered to very-low-income households at prices they can afford to pay. The government knows this, the construction industry knows this, housing experts know this. State and local governments, nonprofit housing organizations, churches, banks, and private business have in recent years mounted a massive effort to increase the stock of affordable housing, but no important federal initiative to provide low-income housing is on the horizon.

Meanwhile the enormous housing subsidy for medium- and high-income families continues. The Internal Revenue code permits homeowners (few low-income families are homeowners) to deduct mortgage interest and property taxes from income in computing their income taxes. In the government's accounts the revenue lost because of these deductions is called a *tax expenditure,* because it has the same effect on the government's financial condition as if the amount forfeited had been spent. This subsidy, which runs well over $30 billion, is far greater than the $14.7 billion expended by the government on housing benefits for low-income households in 1988.[11] Every once in a while the idea surfaces of putting a cap on homeowners' allowable deductions, but any attempt to do so would stir up a monumental political storm.

SPECIAL PROGRAMS FOR THE HOMELESS

In the summer of 1987 Congress passed the Stewart B. McKinney Act authorizing a comprehensive set of programs and benefits for the homeless, including health care, emergency food and shelter, mental health and substance abuse services, transitional housing, social services, education, and job training.

While there is an Interagency Council on the Homeless, the sixteen authorized programs in the categories listed above are administered by several different federal departments.

The basic approach in all the programs seems to be to channel money appropriated for, say, soup kitchens through local governments or nonprofit groups engaged in running soup kitchens. That is, the federal government does not itself run soup kitchens. One coordinating board composed of representatives of the Red Cross, the Salvation Army, and the national charities arms of the three major religious faiths allocates money to private nonprofit organizations and public service agencies that provide emergency food and shelter to the homeless.

In the nation's capital, demonstrators protest the lack of affordable housing across the country.

Other appropriations are distributed to agencies that are trying to help the homeless in these ways: converting buildings into emergency shelters; rehabilitating single-room-occupancy structures (SROs); running soup kitchens and food banks; taking over and distributing donated federal property such as unused buildings, bedding, and clothing; trying to get homeless children into local schools; running programs targeted specifically towards young people who have run away from home.

Despite a universal concern for the homeless, there is considerable difference of opinion in Washington, D.C., about the role the federal government should play in dealing with this problem. Some say there would be no homeless problem of its present dimensions if the federal government had not cut back its appropriations for housing aid and mental health care. Their advice to the federal government is: Don't start a cluster of new programs. Undo the damage you did in the 1980s. Some claim that it is local governments' housing codes and rent control legislation that have intensified the housing crisis and thus increased the ranks of the homeless; therefore change must come in those areas. Some recommend that the federal government should get out of the business of initiating programs for the homeless. Instead they propose block grants of funds with which states can fashion programs to suit their local situations. Some say the federal government should continue to do what it is doing, but with more generous funding. Finally there are those who maintain that special programs for the homeless will simply become a "shelter industry," thus diverting attention from the root causes of homelessness.

MEDICARE

Medicare belongs in this chapter because it is an in-kind transfer program. But it is *not* a social welfare program; it is not a means-tested program. Like Social Security, it is a *social insurance* program. Mandatory payroll deductions during individuals' working lives entitle them to hospital insurance when their Social Security benefits begin; enrollment for additional optional payroll deductions entitles them to medical insurance as well.

Medicare was not designed to be a poverty-reduction program or a program for poor people. Middle-income and wealthy elderly people use it routinely. But it does have a poverty-reducing impact, for it prevents the poverty into which many elderly would fall if their hospital and doctors' bills were not cushioned by the program.

Medicare is an extremely popular program and while everybody deplores the rising costs of medical care, proponents of major shrinkage in Medicare benefits would do well to think carefully about possible political fallout.

5
INVESTING IN PEOPLE: EDUCATION

Consider the John Doe family: father, mother, three children. Its income from the occasional jobs Mr. Doe gets is so far below the poverty threshold for a family of five that the Does cannot meet their basic needs for food, clothing, shelter, and medical care.

Two approaches to helping the Doe family are available. The first has already been described: give them enough cash and in-kind benefits to lift them closer to or even above the poverty threshold. The second is to improve Mr. Doe's position in the labor market so he will earn enough to lift the household out of poverty.

THE CASE FOR HUMAN RESOURCES INVESTMENT

Clearly, making the Doe family independent and self-reliant is more consistent with American values than simply reducing their poverty by cash and in-kind benefits. But is it possible to achieve the self-reliance objective? It depends on the reason or reasons for Mr. Doe's present situation.

Is he a skilled worker or capable of doing only low-level, manual labor? Is he a high school dropout? Can he read and write? Is he a good worker or does his sporadic work history stem from drug or alcohol addiction, poor on-the-job performance, chronic absence and lateness?

It turns out that Mr. Doe is an outstanding argument for investment in human resource programs. A married man with a family, he is an almost risk-free candidate. He was an automobile assembly line worker until his factory closed down. If he is lucky enough to get into a good retraining program, and if he is lucky enough to find a job using his newly acquired skills, he will do just fine. He has the motivation and work habits to be successful.

Now consider thousands of welfare mothers with little education and no work experience, thousands of high school dropouts, thousands of drug addicts or ex-addicts, thousands of ex-offenders newly released from prison, thousands of able-bodied young men who have removed themselves from the labor market for a life of idleness or petty crime. Can their lives be turned around?

Skills-building programs work for some, fail with others. Dropout reversal programs and basic literacy programs help some. Others drop out of the dropout programs. Drug and alcohol rehabilitation programs have had mixed success. Some programs directed specifically at changing people's behavior have reported success, some report that people progress at first, then relapse into old patterns, and some report almost total failure. The only firm conclusion that can be drawn from all the efforts put together is this: It is very difficult to change people.

Then consider that even in good times the private sector may have to be enticed into hiring upgraded people. In bad times changed people will have to compete on unemployment lines with formerly fully employed, productive workers.

Weighed against that picture, income maintenance programs seem like a much easier way to reduce poverty.

But given public and legislators' attitudes, increased appropriations for cash assistance are unlikely in the foreseeable future. Rather, poverty policy will continue to encompass efforts to raise the employability of the poor, to open more widely to them the private sector labor market, and to create public service jobs for them if necessary. This chapter and Chapter 6 will survey what was done along these lines up to the year 1988.

EDUCATION AS A HUMAN RESOURCES INVESTMENT

Which door would you go in for lunch? The one marked:

> cafeteria
> library
> nurse
> principal

That was one of the questions on a test designed to appraise the literacy of seventeen-year-olds. The 13 percent who could not answer questions like that achieved test scores that labeled them "functionally illiterate."[1]

That percentage was disturbing, but even more troubling was the finding that among those functional illiterates were high school graduates as well as high school dropouts. Obviously the schools are not doing their job with total effectiveness. They are losing too many as dropouts and not really teaching, but just passing along, some who stick it out to so-called graduation. Clearly there are young people in school who are not getting the special help they need.

Back in 1964 the Economic Report of President Lyndon Johnson made the optimistic assertion that "if children of poor families can be given skills and motivation, they will not become poor adults."[2] The "if" in that statement is significant. It voices awareness that children brought up in poverty are often educationally disadvantaged. For one thing, poor children are likely to live in areas where the schools are inferior. Books and newspapers, conversation, expectations, encouragement, and role models are often missing in their homes. The stresses of low-income life—crowding, improper diet, worry, untreated illness—may send them to school too burdened physically and emotionally to be ready to learn.

Policy makers in the 1960s War on Poverty were strongly influenced by this linking of poverty with educational disadvantage. Thus it is understandable that when substantial federal aid to education began to flow into the states it was channeled heavily toward programs to provide compensatory (making up for disadvantages) education.

TITLE I PROGRAMS

The largest effort to provide compensatory education is Title I of the 1965 Elementary and Secondary Education Act. Under Title I high-need school districts are identified, then within those districts schools are selected for funding. How Title I money is spent is up to the districts and schools that receive it. In making the selection decisions the percentage of low-achieving children—children one or more years behind grade level—is considered as well as poverty percentages.

Not all needy children are in schools and classes funded for extra help. One early study of Title I showed only 60 percent of the nation's poor children and about 46 percent of low-achieving children receiving Title I help.[3]

On the other hand, the formulas and regulations governing Title I make it difficult to ensure that *only* children who need Title I help get it. In fact, the study mentioned above showed that less than half the children receiving Title I help were poor.

HEAD START

Broad popular support for Head Start, a program for educationally disadvantaged preschool-age children, has continued to protect it from the budget cuts of the 1980s that weakened so many other poverty-reduction programs.

While Head Start programs vary from school district to district, they share common purposes: to get children ready for school, physically and emotionally; to give them the vocabulary that nonpoor children pick up from the day-to-day experiences of family life; to start building learning skills.

Scores in tests taken shortly after the Head Start experience show higher achievement for participants than for comparable nonparticipants in the program. That achievement advantage wanes over the school years, but Head Start youngsters seem less likely than comparable nonparticipants to be held back a grade, or placed in special education classes.

One study attempting to appraise long-term effects of the program found that, at age nineteen, Head Start graduates were more likely than nonparticipants to be employed (although often at low wages) or to be in college or in a vocational training program, and less likely to be on welfare.[4]

Building on the success of Head Start, a Follow Through program helps states offer special services to Head Start children as they move into the primary grades.

BEYOND THE ELEMENTARY YEARS

One group of secondary school programs seeks to identify and motivate students who are likely college material even though their current school records would not ordinarily put them in the ranks of the college bound. A complementary group of programs supports efforts to supply remedial instruction in reading, writing, and study skills to get such students ready to do college work.

One program channels funds to the states to support vocational education for specific problem groups: children from poor families, persons with limited proficiency in English, migrants, and dropouts or potential dropouts.

At the higher education level the Department of Education administers a complex web of seemingly overlapping programs. Their shared purpose is to enable needy students to get an undergraduate or even graduate degree if they are capable of doing the work. Direct government grants, direct government loans, and guaranteed bank loans are available, as is subsidized employment while in college. "Needy" in this context does not mean only individuals from families below the poverty level. Where maximum income levels are specified to define need eligibility, incomes somewhat above poverty levels are often acceptable.

Apparently, in response to the increased need for health professionals, one program offers loans limited to students in schools of dentistry, optometry, podiatry, pharmacy, and veterinary medicine who are "in need" of aid; students in schools of medicine and osteopathy must establish "exceptional financial need." Scholarships are available to first-year students of "exceptional financial need" in all seven specialties.

With so many well-intentioned efforts on the books, it is disheartening to report that something seems to be going wrong with the process of getting educationally disadvantaged secondary students ready for college-level work. The enormous mushrooming of remedial classes on college campuses was an early storm signal; currently rising numbers of college dropouts seem to be another such signal.

This photograph provides a glimpse of the Head Start program in action at the Goldsboro public school in North Carolina.

WHERE DO WE STAND IN OUR EFFORTS
TO REDUCE POVERTY BY EDUCATION?

Recent years have produced a flurry of reports on the state of the nation's schools, all of which have made abundantly plain that it is not only poor children who must be upgraded to higher levels of educational achievement. Compared to students in other developed countries, American students test poorly in science, mathematics, and geography. Not enough students are getting the science and mathematics background to ensure an adequate supply of technologically sophisticated workers. Failure to teach higher-level thinking skills is repeatedly cited as a secondary school shortcoming.

Labor market analysts warn that an increasing percentage of the labor force of the next century must be drawn from today's educationally disadvantaged young people. Unfortunately, no school system has yet come up with a formula that holds those students through the secondary years and sends them out into the labor market with that absolutely basic essential for escape from poverty: a high school diploma earned by educational achievement.

Meanwhile, federal appropriations for programs like Head Start, which have demonstrated some usefulness, are not yet high enough to enable them to serve all the children who need them.

6
INVESTING IN PEOPLE: TRAINING AND EMPLOYMENT PROGRAMS

BEOG, JC, NYC, WIN, JOBS, JTPA, PEP, CETA, CWEP, YEDPA, YIEPP, MDRC*

Few readers will find anything familiar among the acronyms listed above, yet each of them stands for a program that somebody once thought was terrific, a breakthrough, *the answer* to poverty reduction through human resource investment.

TRAINING PROGRAMS

Poverty policy planners of the 1960s could hardly stop with efforts to make schools better. After all, there were thou-

*Basic Educational Opportunity Grants, Job Corps, Neighborhood Youth Corps, Work Incentive Program, Job Opportunities in the Business Sector, Job Training Partnership Act, Public Employment Program, Comprehensive Employment and Training Act, Community Work Experience Plan, Youth Employment and Demonstration Projects Act, Youth Incentive Entitlement Pilot Projects, and Manpower Demonstration Research Corporation.

sands on the streets for whom better schools in the future were irrelevant. School days were over for the unemployed or marginally employed, for the illiterate high school graduates, for the dropouts. Some make-up strategy had to do for those people what school had not done: get them ready for and into the world of work. Each of the acronyms above stands for a program designed to do just that.

The description of training and employment efforts that follows does not attempt to describe, or even mention, all the programs on the list. It merely suggests the variety of strategies that were tried and reports some conclusions about their success.

WORK INCENTIVE PROGRAM (WIN)

In setting up the AFDC program, the Social Security Act of 1935 reflected the then-prevailing consensus that mothers of young children should not be expected to go out to work to support them. By the 1960s, the era of the War on Poverty, an equally strong consensus prevailed that more emphasis should be placed on helping the poor lift themselves out of the situation that had made them dependent on welfare. The Work Incentive Program (WIN), enacted in 1967, reflected that point of view.

All able-bodied AFDC recipients were required to register for the WIN program that every state was thereafter required to create. Exemption was granted to mothers caring for children under six years of age. To free mothers of older children for participation, each state's WIN program had also to make provision for child care.

A wide variety of services was supposed to be offered to participants, including education and training to make them more employable, and job search assistance. But, except in a few states, WIN programs accomplished little. The levels at which they were funded meant that few who registered actually received the services promised.

COMPREHENSIVE EMPLOYMENT AND TRAINING ACT (CETA)

Other legislation of the sixties produced a chaotic mass of overlapping, sometimes conflicting, poverty-reducing programs. To bring some order out of the mess, Congress enacted the 1973 Comprehensive Employment and Training Act (CETA). States, supported by federal funding, were empowered to devise their own combinations of three kinds of training to raise employability levels. For some participants a classroom setting was used to offer basic education and/or occupational training in, say, clerical skills. Other participants who were deemed ready were placed in subsidized private-sector workplaces or public employment and given on-the-job training in the specific skills of low-level jobs. The hope was that trainees would be kept on after the subsidized training period was over.

Participants who lacked even basic work habits—such as getting to a job day after day, getting there on time, working instead of goofing off—were subsidized in private-sector job programs called work experience. The primary goal of these programs was that participants would learn what it means to be a working person. It was hoped that once work behavior was established, skills training could begin.

CETA programs have been very carefully evaluated and the results are somewhat discouraging. Women were found to benefit most from CETA training; men overall made no significant earning gains; the work experience component was judged the least effective.

JOB CORPS

The Job Corps, a 1965 program targeted specifically toward unemployable youth, is generally considered a successful training program. It is expensive because it takes the young people it selects out of their communities into a residential setting where very comprehensive services are provided.

Professional evaluation makes each participant aware of his assets and liabilities as an entrant into the labor market. Then remedial education shores up weaknesses, vocational training builds skills, medical attention clears up health disabilities, citizenship education works on attitudes, and counseling all along the way helps over the hurdles.

Actually it is the dismal record of many other attempts to work with hard-core unemployed youth that makes the Job Corps look good. One study found that two-thirds of those who enter the Corps drop out before completing training and that only one in seven graduates obtained a job using the skills learned in the Corps.[1] But the program takes in young people who are likely candidates for a criminal career, so the evaluators concluded that society saved the money they would have cost in jail; they might have stolen and sold thousands of dollars worth of property; they didn't send anybody into the hospital for care needed after a mugging.

PROGRAMS TARGETED ON A BROADER SAMPLE OF THE UNDERCLASS

Finally, there was a training program directed specifically at the underclass, a five-year, nationwide, *supported-work* experiment that ran from 1975 to 1980. It was initiated by individuals in the private sector who felt that then-existing training and job programs did not adequately serve groups that are hardest to serve. The cooperation of the federal government was enlisted and an outside-the-government corporation was created to run the project, the Manpower Demonstration Research Corporation (MDRC).

Four groups were designated as eligible to participate in the supported-work experiment: mothers who had been on AFDC for a long time, ex-drug addicts, ex-criminal offenders, and school dropouts. Of the 18,000 individuals involved over the five years of the program's life, 30 per-

*Larry Worthy of Rayville, Louisiana, drives a
shingle into the roof of a new dormitory at the
Gary Job Corps Center in San Marcos, Texas. In 1973
officials estimated that it cost almost $5,000
to train each corps member in any one of thirty-
one vocations, ranging from auto mechanic to
electrician, to welder.*

cent had never worked before; 75 percent had dropped out of high school; 90 percent were black or Hispanic.

At some of the twenty-one program sites, participants spent a substantial amount of their time in classrooms, but the basic program involved one year of work at a public or private job, such as rehabilitating housing, maintaining buildings and grounds, clerical work, assisting in day-care centers.

Reports on this project attribute what it was able to accomplish to the fact that it was tightly structured. To give participants the lift of peer support, they worked in crews, closely monitored by supervisors who knew their background and work histories. While at the outset most participants displayed lower than market levels of work behavior and job performance, standards were gradually raised until, at the end, the most successful participants were ready for jobs, got jobs, and held on to them. Many were dropped during the year for irregular attendance or other infractions of rules (the national dropout rate was 70 percent) but good on-the-job performance was rewarded with small bonuses.

Was the program cost, which averaged $5,700 per supported worker, justified? Substantial amounts of quality evaluation produced some reliable findings. For AFDC mothers, benefits were deemed to exceed costs; for dropouts, the program was pronounced a "marginal" success; for the ex-offenders the researchers decided it was impossible to tell whether the program had paid off or not. The verdict on the ex-addict group offers another interesting example of the cost/benefit appraisal process. Their reliance on drugs persisted, but because their program earnings supplied funds to buy the drugs, their criminal activity went down. For that group, benefits were deemed to exceed costs.

In another effort directed at the underclass, the MDRC, in cooperation with the Department of Labor, tried a direct attack on youth unemployment: the Youth Incentive Entitlement Pilot Project. Stay in high school—or come back to high school—the program promised, and we guarantee you a part-time job during the school year and a full-time summer job. At a cost of $4,749 each, about 81,000 young people were involved.

Percentage findings on results look low, but the official verdict on the program was that it did bring back some dropouts who would not otherwise have returned, and it did hold some in school who would otherwise have left.

EMPLOYMENT PROGRAMS

Government can create training programs to prepare workers for the labor market. It can also intervene in the labor market by creating jobs at times or in places where unemployment is unacceptably high. There are two kinds of unemployment. One is called *structural,* the unemployment of disadvantaged, unprepared workers or the unemployment of hitherto employed workers displaced by changes in their industries, such as loss of markets to foreign competitors.

The second kind of unemployment, called *cyclical,* is the unemployment that comes with the recession or depression stages of the business cycle. The government has in the past created jobs to alleviate both kinds of unemployment and thus reduce the rise in poverty associated with unemployment.

JOB CREATION BY THE FEDERAL GOVERNMENT
The Great Depression of the 1930s gave the nation its first demonstration of government's job-creating power. The Works Progress Administration (WPA), one of the government agencies created to cope with the depression, put three million unemployed individuals—one-third of those then unemployed—to work in government-created jobs. By the

early 1940s that program had been phased out but it had demonstrated that public service jobs can be created quickly and need not be mere boondoggling.

After that massive effort, the boom days of World War II and the post-war period took care of unemployment. When recession periods in the 1970s and early 1980s raised the unemployment rate to unacceptable levels, Congress passed a series of job creation laws under which federal funds subsidized thousands of state and local government public service jobs.

INVOLVING THE PRIVATE SECTOR

Can the private sector be persuaded to create jobs to relieve high levels of structural or cyclical unemployment? Yes, if an attractive inducement is offered.

One poverty-reduction program approached private employers this way: Last year you employed 200 workers. Hire four more, that is, increase your payroll to 204 workers, 102 percent of last year's figure. Then keep on hiring and you will receive a tax credit covering the first $6,000 of the wages of the next fifty new employees you take on. Obviously the wages of workers 201, 202, 203, and 204 raised the employer's payroll costs, but workers 205 to 254 were a real bargain. If they were unskilled workers who earned under $6,000 a year, they were better than a bargain. They were free.

Less successful were poverty-reduction efforts to persuade private sector employers to hire specific groups of workers, in other words, to help with structural unemployment. Here is what happened in an attempt to help able-bodied welfare recipients get jobs.

One group of such job seekers were given vouchers certifying that employing them would earn a tax credit; a second group of similar job seekers carried vouchers promising a cash subsidy to employers who took them on. A control group of comparable able-bodied welfare clients were sent out to seek jobs carrying no cash or tax credit bait for potential employers.

Thirteen percent of the voucher holders found jobs, but 21 percent of those carrying no vouchers were successful.[2] More significant: not one employer who took on a worker with a tax credit voucher actually applied for the credit; only one-quarter of the employers entitled to a cash subsidy took the trouble to claim it. Clearly, no breakthrough had been made in techniques to raise the employability of problem job seekers in the private sector.

GOVERNMENT EFFORTS TO STIMULATE ECONOMIC GROWTH

Under the broad umbrella of employment programs belongs a final strategy for poverty reduction: encouraging economic growth. Stimulation of national economic growth is obviously to everyone's advantage. It does indeed create new jobs and it raises the size of the economic pie to be divided up. But it does little for the hard-core unemployed.

Specifically targeted at that group are programs to foster the economic development of high poverty areas. New York State, for example, in cooperation with the federal government, has been working on a plan to attract food processing companies into an area of New York City, one of nineteen so-called Opportunity Zones.[3] These are low-income areas where the very limited amount of business activity offers few jobs to people in the community.

Inducements to attract companies into depressed areas must be substantial. Thus, New York may offer low-interest loans to cover part of the costs of getting businesses started, or it may guarantee loans obtained from private banks. In addition to credit assistance, some programs undertake public works projects that make the target area more attractive.

Proposals for a federal program of such enterprise zones include as bait some easing of federal regulations applying to specific industries, as well as tax credits. Jobs, specifically jobs for the poor, are what is hoped for from targeted economic development, but so far few substantial success stories have been reported.

AN APPRAISAL

One broad conclusion must be drawn from this brief review of training and employment programs that aim to reduce poverty by raising the earnings of poor people: their poverty-reducing potential is modest at best. As the program descriptions have revealed, there are two basic reasons for their limited impact. First, they can serve only the employable poor. Consider the significance of that limitation. One informed estimate suggests that about 40 percent of the structurally unemployed cannot be made employable by any program at reasonable cost.[4] Second, even successful training programs have prepared few for jobs that offer better than poverty wages.

But there is another side to the coin. Many would argue this way: What if many training and employment programs do not have a poverty-reducing impact commensurate with their cost? (Some very expensive weapons systems have turned out to be duds.) They put some people to work and, in the view of most Americans, getting people to work is better than letting them not work, even though it would cost the government less to give them, as welfare, the amount they earn as workers.

7
WELFARE REFORM I: GETTING TOUGH WITH ABSENT FATHERS

By the mid-1980s the social welfare system of the United States was characterized by these essential features:

- fairly satisfactory attention to the needs of the elderly
- fairly generous provision for the totally and permanently disabled
- very little assistance for able-bodied men and women if single, or married but childless
- an elaborate if not overly generous system, AFDC, to meet the needs of single parents (almost always mothers) with children

The first two features enjoyed general acceptance. The third troubled few. The fourth, which in the public mind was ''welfare,'' had never won warm public support. Then in the mid-1980s it came under attack as a contributing cause of the problems of the ghettos. Many agreed with the critical journalist who charged:

*To women, the AFDC system seems to say,
"Have a kid and the state will take care of you—
as long as you don't live with the father." To
men, it says, "Father children and the state will
take care of them."* [1]

BACKGROUND FOR WELFARE REFORM

As we have seen, research evidence demonstrates that welfare benefits do not cause out-of-wedlock births; teen-age girls have babies for far more complex reasons than to get on welfare. But in the 1980s it was an appealing antiwelfare argument. Equally appealing was the argument that even if welfare does not *cause* out-of-wedlock births and single-parent households, it is the support system that sustains them. Thus an antiwelfare public mood stimulated support for welfare reform in the 1980s. But more fundamental concerns bolstered that support.

The nation's economic condition had changed. From the early 1970s on, the economic status of workers has been less rosy than it was in the previous two decades. As Figure 7-1 shows, the median wage of full-time, year-round workers peaked in 1973 and, despite a rising trend that began in the mid-1980s, the median has not yet returned to the level of that peak year.

One response to that change in workers' fortunes was the entrance of more women into the labor market. With the help of these additional contributors, real (that is, adjusted for price changes) median *family* income recovered during the 1980s to its 1973 peak, as Figure 7-2 shows.

During the same years that workers' fortunes and families' work patterns went through the changes just described, another development made demand for welfare reform virtually inevitable. Between 1973 and 1987 the number of female-headed families grew by 3.6 million, a 66.4 percent increase.[2] Lest there be any misunderstanding, it must be emphasized that there are millions of fe-

92

Figure 7-1. Median Earnings of Year-Round, Full-Time Workers (1960–1987)

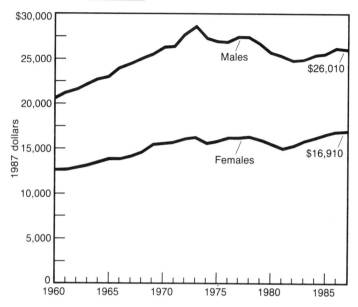

Source: U.S. Department of Commerce, Bureau of the Census, Current Population Reports, Population Profile of the United States: 1989, Special Studies, Series P–23, No. 159, Issued April 1989, p.33

male-headed families that are far from poor. But as Figure 7-3 illustrates, it is the poverty percentage among female-headed families *with children* that is alarming.

Inevitably, along with the explosive growth of female-headed families with children came an explosive growth in the AFDC caseload. By 1988 one out of eight families with children under eighteen was on welfare. In 1960 the ratio had been one out of thirty-three. Incidentally that surge in the welfare rolls is further rebuttal of the contention that generous welfare benefits cause the formation of single-parent families. From the early 1970s into the 1980s, the years of burgeoning welfare rolls, inflation was cutting the value of unadjusted welfare benefits by more than 30 percent.[3]

Figure 7-2. Median Family Income, by Race and Hispanic Origin (1970–1987)

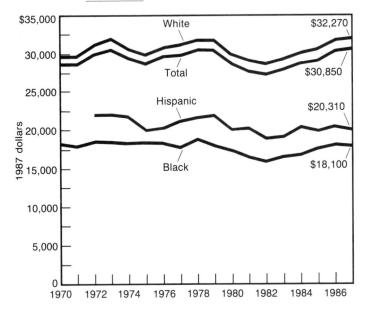

Source: U.S. Department of Commerce. Bureau of the Census. Current Population Reports. Population Profile of the United States: 1989. Special Studies, Series P-23, No. 159. Issued April 1989, p.32.

Figure 7-3. Families in Poverty

	Number in category	Number in poverty	Percent in poverty
		(millions)	
All families	65.8	6.9	10.4
Married couple families	52.1	2.9	5.6
Female householder, no husband present, related children under 18	7.4	3.3	44.7

94

Thus, two trends were going on at the same time. More and more middle-income women were finding it essential to work to maintain their standard of living. More and more young women, with their children, were establishing households maintained by the welfare system without their working.

Furthermore, along with the *actual* surge in single-parent families came dire predictions of what lay ahead. By 1988 it was estimated that over one-half of the children born in the United States thereafter would, at some time in their first eighteen years, live in a mother-only family. The significance of that estimate in terms of poverty and welfare dependency was inescapable.[4]

Welfare reform became inevitable and in October 1988 the Family Support Act became law. As set forth in the law itself its purpose is:

> *to revise the AFDC program to emphasize work, child support, and family benefits, to amend title IV of the Social Security Act to encourage and assist needy children and parents under the new program to obtain the education, training, and employment needed to avoid long-term welfare dependence . . .*[5]

Basically, the law sends two messages. To welfare mothers: You cannot expect to remain on welfare indefinitely. Even though you have young children you must prepare to free yourself from welfare dependence. To absent fathers: If you father a child you must help support that child. Don't try to evade that responsibility. We will find you.

WHY THE CHILD SUPPORT SYSTEM
NEEDED STRENGTHENING

The Family Support Act's admonition to fathers seems like such a commonsense as well as moral position that the actual child support situation in the 1980s is difficult to

*In 1988 three-quarters of all poor black families
were headed by females. Lois Kimber is a twenty-three-
year-old unwed mother of four who hasn't worked in
seven years but is eager to find a job. She is
seen here enjoying a book with her son in their
trailer home in Tunica, Mississippi.*

understand. In 1985 there were 4,381,000 women with children under twenty-one who were entitled to child support payments under separation or divorce agreements or court awards. Of that number, 48.2 percent were receiving what they were entitled to; 25.8 percent were receiving partial payments; 26.0 percent were receiving nothing.[6] Several studies have suggested that absent fathers were annually evading about $25 billion in child support payments.[7]

The situation for out-of-wedlock mothers was much worse. Fewer than 12 percent of the fathers involved in these cases were paying anything at all toward the care of the children they had fathered.[8]

CHILD SUPPORT ENFORCEMENT PROGRAM (CSE)

Clearly earlier legislation to deal with child support delinquency had not worked. In 1975 an amendment to the Social Security Act had created a federal office of Child Support Enforcement and required each state to establish a similar agency to serve AFDC families and non-AFDC families who asked for its assistance. These state agencies help to locate absent parents, establish paternity, obtain child support orders, and collect payments. A Parent Locator Service was also created, with access to Social Security earnings records and Internal Revenue Service tax records.

Inclusion of non-AFDC families in the CSE program was an attempt to prevent families on the edge of financial difficulties from going on welfare. The hope was that if CSE could find missing parents and get child support payments flowing into those families, then states and the federal government would avoid substantial welfare costs.

LOCATING ABSENT PARENTS
Several provisions of the Family Support Act strengthened CSE's ability to locate missing fathers and establish pa-

ternity. Most applicants for AFDC have traditionally been required to name the fathers of their children—refusal to do so can mean denial of benefits. That penalty is rarely invoked, however, because the number of applicant mothers who do not give the information requested is less than one percent.

Under the new law, states are required to obtain the social security numbers of both parents at the time of a child's birth. With this information, access to Social Security and tax data, and computers that can search public data banks from credit files to rosters of prison inmates, CSE offices are becoming increasingly efficient at tracking down missing parents. If a located parent denies paternity, the new law requires states to use blood- and genetic-typing tests to resolve the issue.

If states lag in their parent-locating efforts, a penalty looms. The law provides for reduction of a state's AFDC matching funds if it does not find and establish paternity of a required percentage of its missing fathers case load. If CSE offices perform their functions efficiently, there is a reward: a bonus from the federal government that can go as high as 10 percent of their CSE collections if they have a good record on the costs of collections compared to the amount of collections.

OBTAINING AND ENFORCING
CHILD SUPPORT ORDERS

Once a missing father is found, a child support order must be negotiated. In the past, states have had guidelines for the use of judges and others empowered to make child support awards. But the guidelines have not been binding and many such awards have seemed more concerned with the father's ability to support himself than with his obligations as a parent. "Judge shopping" for a jurist known for his kindness to fathers was not uncommon.

The new law requires that states enact guidelines and make them virtually mandatory upon those setting awards.

The law further requires that the guidelines be reviewed every four years. If New York State's new guidelines are typical, even poor fathers will not escape some obligation. In that state, a noncustodial parent whose income is below the poverty level nevertheless has to pay at least $25 a month in child support.

Finally, starting in 1993, every child support award must be reviewed every three years to be sure that "appropriate" amounts are being collected from the noncustodial parent.

By far the most important enforcement weapon is the provision for mandatory payroll deduction of child support payments. Under the new law employers must withhold from paychecks payments due to AFDC families under child support orders, and forward them to the appropriate CSE offices.

The AFDC mother does not get these payments because applicants for AFDC are required to sign over their rights to child support to the state. Any child support payments an AFDC mother receives directly, that is without CSE intervention, are deducted from her benefits (except for the first $50 received in any one month).

Payments retained by a CSE office are applied on the state's financial records against AFDC benefits paid. Payments received on behalf of non-AFDC families are forwarded to them.

Until the year 1994, mandatory withholding applies only to AFDC families but on January 1, 1994, it will go into effect for all individuals who are under a court order to make child support payments, unless the two parents involved waive CSE intervention.

A recent newspaper report suggests that even judges seem to be getting into the spirit of rigorous enforcement of parental responsibilities.

As a result of the new law, judges say they are demanding larger support payments and are

quicker to strip delinquent parents, usually fa-
thers, of their property instead of trying to col-
lect back payments. "I take away their rings
and empty their wallets right in court . . ." [9]

IS THE STRENGTHENED CSE PROGRAM EFFECTIVE?

The record of the CSE program indicates that it is effective in increasing child support payments and thus reducing the costs to the states and federal government of welfare dependency. A 1989 congressional study indicated that child support payments collected by state CSE offices helped 200,000 families leave the welfare system.

Its usefulness as a poverty-reducing strategy, however, is limited by the prevailing low level of child support awards. Even with mandatory guidelines and zealous judges, significant numbers of single-parent families are unlikely to be lifted out of poverty by CSE efficiency.

In the opinion of many poverty experts a much more basic principle will have to be written into child support law. Some kind of government subsidy will be necessary if there is to be any substantial reduction of the shocking percentage of children living in poverty, with all the implications that childhood poverty carries for the future well-being of the nation.

One expert suggests a Child Support Assurance Plan that would work like this: A minimum level of child support would have to be decided upon, say $150 per month per child. Assume that Charles Needy is subject to a child support order under which he must pay his wife $200 per month toward the care of their two children. Mr. Needy's employer deducts $200 from his paycheck each month and sends that amount to the state CSE office. That office adds $100 of government funds and sends Mrs. Needy a check for $300.

The proponent of this plan maintains that if (1) such a Child Support Assurance Plan were in effect, (2) Medicaid eligibility were extended to cover low-income working poor families, and (3) the minimum wage were higher, then welfare for mothers working part time could be eliminated.[10]

Others maintain that the poverty-reduction impact of AFDC can be strengthened only if it becomes a national program with a uniform minimum level of benefits.

Those who take a longer-range view, urge this approach: Let's try to get the word through to young men that if they father a child they will be required to contribute to the support of that child for years to come. The message just might be a deterrent to the birth of children doomed to lives in poverty.

8

WELFARE REFORM II: GETTING YOUNG MOTHERS OFF WELFARE

Nancy K. Murphy, a twenty-eight-year-old single mother, was earning $160 a week as a children's photographer in shopping malls near a small city in Minnesota. The company she worked for has a good benefits program and she had the use of a company car. Her salary was low enough to qualify her for the state's child-care subsidy program under which she received $200 a month. The actual cost of care for her 16-month-old son, Spencer, was often as high as $300 but she was managing very well.

Then came the Family Support Act of 1988 and Minnesota found itself under rigorous new requirements to provide child care subsidies under a new federal program. ''We had to find the money, so we had to kick working poor folks off child-care subsidies,'' an official in the Minnesota Department of Human Services explained.

"Some of them quit their jobs and went back on welfare." Nancy Murphy was one of them.[1]

That is not the way the Family Support Act was supposed to work, of course. Its purpose was to get AFDC mothers off welfare, not to drive working poor mothers into the welfare system. But Nancy Murphy's story was used to make a point: It is extremely difficult to enact and administer social welfare legislation that achieves intended goals without creating unanticipated side effects or opening up unforeseen loopholes.

Over the years change after change has been made in the AFDC program in an attempt to minimize its welfare-dependence-building effects. That these attempts had not been successful in eliminating long-term dependency is evidenced by the 1980s demand for welfare reform and passage of the Family Support Act of 1988.

A NEW APPROACH TO BUILDING SELF-SUFFICIENCY

This chapter will describe the training and employment provisions of the Family Support Act designed to get young mothers off welfare. It will be organized under the flaws in the system they are supposed to correct. As this picture of the second major part of the act emerges, readers can make their own assessments as to how well its weaknesses have been strengthened; they can make their own predictions about side effects that may emerge—a Nancy Murphy situation, for example—and about the loopholes that may weaken the act's effectiveness.

The text of the Family Support Act uses the term "parents" in referring to AFDC recipients but our treatment will use "mothers" instead, since the overwhelming majority of the single parents are single mothers and there is no question about the act being directed at them.

TOO MANY AFDC MOTHERS WERE EXEMPT FROM PREVIOUS TRAINING/EMPLOYMENT PROGRAMS

Under the WIN program, welfare mothers of *school-age* children had to register for training and employment, a departure from the traditional position that society must support mothers who are raising young children so they can stay home and care for their youngsters. Under later legislation, states were permitted to require workfare for mothers of children from three to six and a few states did introduce such a requirement.

But by the 1980s American public opinion was ready to make a work requirement for mothers of young children mandatory. Since the economic crunch of the late 1970s and early 1980s, nonwelfare mothers had been leaving their preschool children and going off to work. Why shouldn't welfare mothers do the same? Thus the Family Support Act contained these provisions:

1. Each state is required to establish a Job Opportunities and Basic Skills (JOBS) program.
2. All able-bodied mothers whose youngest child is at least *three* must be enrolled in that program.
3. States that wish to bring more mothers into their JOBS programs may require enrollment if the youngest child is at least *one*.
4. A JOBS enrollee under age twenty who has not been graduated from high school or earned an equivalency diploma must work toward that objective *full time* no matter how young her youngest child is. An enrollee aged eighteen or nineteen who fails to make good progress in school or who is deemed an inappropriate candidate for further schooling will be required to enter a training or employment program.
5. The extent of JOBS participation required of mothers with children under six is limited to twenty hours per

week. That limitation is consistent with the realities of women's participation in the labor force. While it is true that two-thirds of married mothers with young children are in the labor force, under one-third of them work full time.

6. Failure to participate in the JOBS program may result in loss of the mother's share of AFDC benefits and possible routing of her children's benefits through a third party.

7. To ensure that states provide enough resources to serve significant percentages of JOBS enrollees, quotas for participation are written into the act:

   • In 1990 and 1991, 7 percent enrolled must be participating; 11 percent in 1992 and 1993; 15 percent in 1994; 20 percent by 1995.
   • Federal matching funds will be reduced if these quotas are not met.

8. States must "guarantee" child care if such care is necessary for an individual to participate in the JOBS program. The state can do this by providing its own child-care facilities, by contracting with private child-care providers, by vouchers, or by advance or reimbursement payments for the child-care arrangements mothers make for themselves. The federal government will match state expenditures for child care provided they are within these limits: $175 per month per child; $200 per month for children under two.[2]

PREVIOUS TRAINING/EMPLOYMENT PROGRAMS FOR AFDC MOTHERS WERE TOO NARROW

The Family Support Act requires that each state's JOBS program offer participants these four services:

1. education

   • to achieve a high school diploma, or
   • to achieve basic literacy, or

- to achieve a higher level of proficiency in English as the participant's second language

2. job skills training
3. job readiness activities
4. job development and placement service, which includes working with the private sector to find jobs

In addition to those four services, any two of these programs must be offered:

- group and individual job-search training
- on-the-job training
- subsidized jobs in the private sector, that is, jobs for which the state would supply the wages paid to the mother by the employer, those wages replacing her AFDC benefits. The hope here is that the private sector employer will keep the worker on after the period of subsidy ends.
- a work experience program under which participants work off their benefits in community service jobs (workfare)

The act specifically mandates that each participant be assigned a counselor who will custom-design a program from the state's menu of six program offerings, a program that will make her employable and put her to work.

PREVIOUS TRAINING/EMPLOYMENT PROGRAMS DID NOT FOCUS ON THOSE MOST IN NEED OF THE PROGRAMS

The WIN program, it has been noted, was inadequately funded; too few enrollees were served. Furthermore, the law that created WIN specifically directed that "employability potential" was to be taken into consideration in choosing those to be served with the limited resources available. In other words, the people most likely to be attractive to employers were to be made increasingly employable.

In sharp contrast to this, the Family Support Act lists the target groups on which the states must concentrate their efforts:

- long-term recipients of AFDC
- mothers without a high school diploma or recent work experience
- families about to lose welfare because the youngest child is approaching the age of eighteen.

The Act also includes quotas and financial penalties for failure to comply with these prescriptions.

THE PERIOD AFTER A WORKING AFDC MOTHER WENT OFF THE WELFARE ROLLS PRESENTED SERIOUS PROBLEMS

The Social Security Act required that any income received by an AFDC recipient be deducted from her benefits. While that requirement was eased by ''disregards'' (portions of income *not* counted and deducted), eventually some workers reached the point where their counted earnings exceeded their benefits and they were dropped from the rolls. They then had to pay their own child-care expenses and their families lost Medicaid coverage.

Under the Family Support Act, when a working mother loses her AFDC benefits because her counted income has reached the eligibility ceiling she will continue to receive child support assistance for a year. The limits remain $175 per month per child ($200 for children under two); the actual amount of assistance given will be determined by the mother's ability to pay. Medicaid coverage of the family is guaranteed for a year.

MANY STATES HAD NO AFDC-UP PROGRAM

The Family Support Act requires all states (28 already had the program) to extend AFDC to needy two-parent families in which the principal earner is unemployed (AFDC-UP). To ease the burden on states thus forced into the program, they are required to pay benefits for only six months out of any twelve-month period. Medicaid coverage, however, must be offered to such families year-round.

To ensure that AFDC-UP families do something in return for the benefits they will receive, participation quotas are specified. At least one parent must be involved·in a part-time work program in 40 percent of those families by 1994, in 75 percent of those families by 1997.

SHOULD YOUNG SINGLE MOTHERS LIVE ON THEIR OWN?

The AFDC program encouraged young single mothers to set up their own households rather than remain with parents or other relatives. Many felt that this policy was impractical, that minors should either be required to remain in their homes or live in an alternative setting where there would be supportive adults and some control over the minors' way of life.

The Family Support Act provided that states may, as a condition for eligibility, require that a mother under eighteen who has never married live with a parent, legal guardian, or other adult relative, or in a foster home, or maternity home or some other acceptable group-living arrangement.

TWO KEY ISSUES RAISED BY THE FAMILY SUPPORT ACT OF 1988

CHILD CARE

The Family Support Act makes two major child-care commitments: child care during the period of education and training; child-care benefits during the transition out of welfare dependence.

Every major piece of legislation is amplified by "regulations" drawn up by the administering bureaucracy. The regulations accompanying the Family Support Act deliberately avoid telling welfare mothers what arrangements they should make for the care of their children. Stressing that day-care centers are not the only acceptable option, the regulations state: "In many cases, informal care provided by trusted friends or family members is the parents' preferred source of care."[3]

That statement is certainly borne out by the Census Bureau's 1984–85 report on child-care practices of mothers. Of the 8.2 million preschool age (0–4) children covered by the bureau's study:

- 1.9 million were cared for in day-care centers or preschools
- 31 percent were supervised in their own homes
- 37 percent were cared for in another person's home
- 8 percent were cared for by the mother herself while at work (mothers employed as workers in private households or as child-care workers, for example)[4]

However, as one knowledgeable commentator on the regulations pointed out, many of the mothers who are the target population of the act are teenagers. Their "trusted friends" are likely to be teenagers who are supposed to be in school. Their aunts and grandmothers are well under retirement age and likely to be workers themselves.

Every analysis of the Family Support Act identifies the child-care issue as one on which its success will hinge. Where will the states get the funds they must invest? If states falter, will the federal government do more than it is currently promising to do? And even if funds for child-care fees are forthcoming, where are the estimated 1.5 million new day-care slots to come from? Where are the professionals to run them?

MANDATORY WORK
Welfare rights activists assert that it is unfair to train mothers for, and place them in, low-income, dead-end jobs.

But an unpleasant reality of the labor market is that most of the jobs welfare mothers will be qualified to take after they have met the education and training requirements of the new law are not going to be good jobs. In fact, as one labor expert, Eli Ginzberg of Columbia University, has pointed out, 40 percent of the jobs people hold in today's labor market are low-wage, dead-end jobs. Furthermore, while society has many tasks to be done—the infrastructure repaired, libraries kept open longer—not too many people can be put into public service jobs without running into opposition from public employee unions.

Then there is the thorny question of workfare. Should the Family Support Act have made workfare programs an acceptable component of JOBS programs? Should anybody be made to work for his or her AFDC benefits? Feelings run high between those who are "soft" or "hard" on workfare. Held up for derision are programs that require work but do not really enforce the requirement. Under California's workfare law, for example, welfare recipients are exempt from the workfare requirement if they are "seriously dependent upon alcohol or drugs" or if they have "an emotional or mental problem," "legal difficulties," or "a severe family crisis." They don't have to accept a job that requires more than an hour's travel from their homes; they must be offered a choice of day-care services.[5]

Massachusetts Welfare Commissioner Charles Atkins's position, "I think workfare is slavery," is typical of a "soft" position on workfare. In contrast, here is a "hard" position:

> . . . what's most important is not whether sweeping streets or cleaning buildings helps Betsy Smith, single teenage parent and high school dropout, learn skills that will help her find a private sector job. It is whether the prospect of sweeping streets and cleaning buildings for a welfare grant will deter Betsy Smith from hav-

ing the illegitimate child that drops her out of school and onto welfare in the first place—or, failing that, whether the sight *of Betsy Smith sweeping streets after having her illegitimate child will discourage her younger sisters and neighbors from doing as she did.*[6]

UNFINISHED BUSINESS

The Family Support Act did not mandate two changes that have been urged by poverty experts. It did not make AFDC a national system with a national minimum level of benefits, and it did not authorize states to set time limits on the receipt of AFDC benefits, a proposal that even many liberals are in favor of. In other words, it did not authorize states to say to an able-bodied welfare mother after, say, thirty-six months of benefits: You have not found a job for yourself. You have not accepted private sector jobs we found for you. There is a public service job open in Department X for which you are qualified. Show up for that job and you will be paid. Your AFDC benefits are terminated.

This posture would transform AFDC into a temporary, emergency support system. Those genuinely unable to work would be cared for under other programs. The government would become the employer of last resort so there would always be a public service job that would prevent destitution. Welfare dependence as a way of life would end.

Antonio Leon, a welfare recipient who must work for his bimonthly check, pulls weeds for the New York City Parks Department.

113

Is the Family Support Act worth all the attention we have given it? A Congressional Budget Office report of January 1989 predicts that by 1993 the law will have removed only about 50,000 families from the national AFDC caseload. But Senator Daniel Moynihan of New York, probably the Family Support Act's most influential sponsor, while admitting that it will take a decade to assess its effectiveness, added this plea:

> *It's what the governors asked for, and most of the states are just roaring ahead. . . . Whether other people get in the spirit of this legislation and try to make it work or sit around and complain about it remains to be seen. But there will not be another bill in this century, so let's do the best thing for the children.*[7]

9
THE WAR THAT
IS NOT OVER

August 20, 1989, was the twenty-fifth anniversary of the proclamation of a war on poverty, a war committed "to eliminate the paradox of poverty in the midst of plenty." [1]

As figure 9-1 shows, substantial progress was made toward that goal until 1973. But then came a distressing rise in poverty and the ground lost in those recession years has not yet been retaken. Furthermore, behind the unacceptable poverty rate loom the sobering specifics: over 12 million children are living in poverty, with all the educational disadvantage that implies for them and for the nation's future; there are over 30 million people with no protection against the hazards of illness; millions of elderly with no protection against the costs of nursing home care in their final years; the highest teenage birth rate among the developed nations of the world; increasing distortion in the composition of the nation's families.

Can we take hope from the fact that there are some new weapons for the war on poverty? Having discovered the magic of using the tax code instead of the welfare bureaucracy, can we look forward to the Earned Income Tax

Figure 9-1. Poverty Rates (1959-1988)

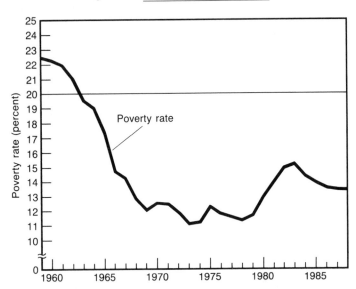

Source: U.S. Library of Congress, Congressional Research Service, Progress Against Poverty in the United States (1959 to 1987), CRS Report for Congress by Thomas Gabe, March 24, 1989, Report No. 89-211 EPW.

Credit further lifting the fortunes of the working poor? Dare we be encouraged that conservatives and liberals, instead of sticking to positions etched in stone, are talking to each other about tax credits for children, the children of non-working as well as of working and welfare mothers; that they are talking about health insurance; that they are talking about—even though they did not get it into the Family Support Act—a time limit on welfare benefits that might really break the back of welfare dependence? Is the grass roots attack on the housing shortage in the face of federal inertia a harbinger of broadened public support for action on social issues? How discouraged must we be that the unequal distribution of income that is the root cause of poverty continues, in fact worsens?

How do knowledgeable, concerned public figures and academics react as they look back on the interval between the 1960s and the present—and look ahead? Here is how Gary Burtless of the Brookings Institution feels:

In view of Americans' deep-seated beliefs [that so long as legal remedies are enforced to ensure that the market race is fair, the rich and the poor will get what they deserve], there are scant grounds for optimism that the lot of the nation's poor will soon be radically improved. The steep rise in social welfare spending between 1960 and 1980 substantially raised the well-being of many poor families, and these improvements ought not be lightly dismissed. But much of the increased spending was concentrated on the lucky poor insured by our social insurance programs—the aged, the infirm, and the insured unemployed. Most of the remainder was devoted to in-kind benefits that raised specific forms of consumption, but not the money incomes of the poor. In the recent past, government initiative to reduce poverty has come to a halt and may even have been reversed.[2]

In sharp contrast, Hyman Bookbinder, who was executive officer of President Lyndon B. Johnson's Task Force on Poverty in 1964, looks back and ahead in these terms:

Can we afford a renewed war on poverty? Is it even thinkable at a time of huge Federal deficits?

First, we cannot afford not to resume the war. One way or another, the problems will remain expensive. Somehow, we will provide for the survival needs of the poorest: welfare, food stamps, beds and roofs for the homeless, Med-

117

icaid. The fewer poor there are, the fewer the relief problems. Getting people out of poverty is the most cost-effective public investment.

Second, if the additional public funds required for adequate education and training and housing programs cannot come from increased or diverted Federal funds, taxes must be raised.[3]

Then Bookbinder nudges our collective conscience with a word from an even earlier antipoverty warrior:

In 1939, a quarter century before Presidents John F. Kennedy and Johnson declared war on poverty, Franklin D. Roosevelt gave us a sound basis for judging our national character. "The test of our progress," he said, "is not whether we add more to the abundance of those who already have much; it is whether we do enough for those who have too little."

Twenty-five years from today, will we be able to say we have met that test?[4]

GLOSSARY

Absolute standard of poverty: specific income levels used to identify poor households.

AFDC (Aid to Families with Dependent Children): a federal/state income maintenance program initiated in 1935 as part of the Social Security Act.

Aggregate income: income earned from all sources.

Boondoggling: work of little or no value.

Cash transfers: payments by government to individuals for which no product is delivered or service rendered.

Categorically needy: persons presumed to be eligible for Medicaid because they are receiving other types of public assistance such as AFDC or SSI.

Census Bureau: an agency in the Commerce Department whose responsibilities include (1) taking a census of the population every ten years, (2) collecting, tabulating, and publishing a wide variety of statistical data about the people and the economy of the nation to serve as the basis for development and evaluation of economic and social programs.

CETA (Comprehensive Employment and Training Act):

legislation that provided federal funding for state programs that offered a variety of training programs to raise the employability of welfare recipients.

Child Support Assurance Plan: a proposal that court-ordered child-support payments be supplemented by government cash transfers large enough to ensure that all custodial parents receive a mandated monthly minimum per child.

Child Support Enforcement (CSE) program: a program designed to strengthen the collection from absent fathers of court-ordered child-support payments.

Child-support guidelines: schedules of appropriate levels of child support that states must formulate and courts must use in handing down child-support orders.

Compensatory education: efforts to help the educationally disadvantaged catch up with students free from such handicaps.

Cost/benefit analysis: a method of evaluating training and education programs in which the cost per participant is compared to the value to society of the participant's changed behavior.

Counted income: that part of a family's income that is used as the basis for determining eligibility for certain need-based programs (such as Food Stamps), arrived at by deducting allowances for unusual expenses from total money income.

Culture of poverty: ways of thinking, acting, and believing that may develop among an isolated poverty population.

Current Population Survey: the Census Bureau's annual March collection of data from a large representative sample of the nation's households concerning income, education, and work experience of household members during the preceding year.

Cyclical unemployment: joblessness caused by a period of recession or depression.

Disregards: allowances granted to working AFDC recipients that limit the extent to which their earnings are deducted from their AFDC benefits.

Distribution of income: the way in which the aggregate income of all households is divided among them, conventionally computed by arranging household incomes in ascending sequence, dividing the sequence into five equal groups of households, and expressing the total income received by each fifth as a percentage of the aggregate income.

Earned Income Tax Credit (EITC): a cash transfer or credit-against-owed-income-tax that is available to wage earners with children whose income does not exceed $19,340.

Economic growth: a rise in the real value of the goods and services produced by the economy.

Economy Food Plan (sometimes called Thrifty Food Plan): an eating plan designed by the Department of Agriculture for low-income families in order to determine the minimum expenditure for food that would, for the short term, provide adequate nutrition for a family of four.

Educationally disadvantaged: children and young people whose home and neighborhood environments include conditions that are assumed to limit their ability to learn.

Emergency Assistance: a federal public assistance program under which states receive 50 percent reimbursement for cash and in-kind transfers to families with children in emergencies created by natural disasters or domestic crises.

Employability potential: the degree to which an individual is deemed likely to be employed, a factor sometimes considered in choosing participants for training programs.

Enterprise zones: See Opportunity zones.

Family: two or more persons related by birth, adoption, or marriage and living together.

Family Support Act: legislation designed to (1) change the AFDC program in ways that will discourage long-term welfare dependency, and (2) strengthen enforcement of the child support obligations of absent fathers.

Federal housing programs: public assistance programs under which needy families receive housing assistance in the form of low rents in public housing, controlled rents in federally subsidized private housing, or rent supplements paid by the federal government to owners of private housing.

Fiscal year: an accounting period of twelve months. The federal government's fiscal year is October 1 through September 30.

Follow Through: a federal program that provides special services to Head Start participants as they move into the primary grades.

Food Stamp program: a federal public assistance program under which needy individuals and families receive stamps that serve as currency for the purchase of food.

Full-time work: fifty weeks of thirty-five-hours-per-week employment.

Functional illiterate: an individual whose reading and writing ability is so limited as to affect his or her ability to handle many of the routines of daily life.

General Assistance: the term used in many states to cover need-based cash transfers dispensed through local and state welfare systems to meet situations not covered under targeted programs.

Head Start: a federal program that seeks to improve the school achievement of educationally disadvantaged children by giving them a preschool learning experience designed to improve their readiness for conventional schooling.

Homelessness: the condition that afflicts individuals and families unable to find housing they can afford.

Household: one or more persons occupying a housing unit.

Human resource programs: programs directed toward increasing the employability and earning power of individuals applying for or receiving public assistance.

Income maintenance programs: programs under which cash payments by the government supplement incomes diminished by retirement, unemployment, or disability.

Income tax: a tax on the earnings of individuals or businesses.

Inequality of income distribution: the situation that exists when the percentage of total income received by the lowest income-earning groups in a population is substantially lower then the percentage earned by the highest-earning group of that population.

Inflation: a general rise in the price level.

In-kind transfers: noncash, need-based benefits such as medical care, food, housing assistance.

Internal Revenue Code: regulations governing the preparation and filing of income tax returns.

Job Corps: a rigorous training program for high-risk youths offered at away-from-home residential or camp sites.

JOBS (Job Opportunities and Basic Skills program): the education and training program for able-bodied recipients of AFDC benefits that states are required by the Family Support Act to establish.

Low-income families: those families whose income is substantially below the national median income for families of their size.

Mandatory payroll deductions: a method for ensuring payment of child-support obligations under which employers are required to deduct court-ordered payments from employees' paychecks.

Matching funds: federal grants to states that equal the states' expenditures for designated programs.

McKinney Act: legislation enacted in 1987 to set up programs and benefits for the homeless.

Meals-on-wheels: prepared meals delivered by local social welfare organizations to the homes of elderly or disabled persons.

Means of subsistence: resources for maintaining life.

Median income: that income which is the midpoint of a range of incomes; half the incomes are below the median, half above.

Medicaid: a federal/state program that provides medical, hospital, and nursing home care to persons who meet the standards of need established in federal and state legislation.

Medically needy: individuals whose medical expenses reduce their incomes to a level that makes them eligible for Medicaid.

Medicare: a social insurance program, funded in part by employer/employee contributions, that provides substantial coverage of the hospital expenses of the elderly and of the medical expenses of those Medicare-eligible persons who choose to buy that additional protection.

Middle income: incomes at, somewhat above, or somewhat below the national median income.

Minimum wage: the lowest hourly wage that may legally be paid by employers subject to local, state, or federal minimum wage legislation.

National School Lunch program: a federal/state social welfare program designed to ensure that nutritionally satisfactory lunches are available to needy schoolchildren, free or at below-market cost.

OASDI (Old Age, Survivors, and Disability Insurance): OASI plus income maintenance payments to previously employed but permanently disabled workers.

OASI (Old Age and Survivors Insurance): the social insurance program under which income maintenance benefits are paid to retired workers and their eligible survivors.

Opportunity zones: low-income areas to which governments attempt to attract business and industry, hence jobs, by offering incentives such as credit assistance or relaxation of regulations.

Per capita income: the aggregate money income received by all the people of a nation divided by the population of the nation.

Poverty: the condition of being poor with respect to money, goods, or means of subsistence.

Poverty income guidelines: the income levels used by the Department of Health and Human Services in determining eligibility for the welfare programs it administers.

Poverty thresholds: the income levels used by the Census Bureau that determine poverty status.

Private sector: businesses owned and operated by individuals, partnerships, and corporations.

Progressive tax: a tax in which the rate assessed or burden of payment increases as income increases.

Public assistance: cash or other kinds of benefits dispensed by governments to meet the needs of its least fortunate citizens.

Public service employment: jobs on a government payroll.

Public welfare system: the arrangements through which a government dispenses public assistance.

Real income: money income adjusted to reflect price changes so that year-to-year income comparisons are meaningful.

Regressive tax: a tax in which the rate assessed or burden of payment decreases as income increases.

Relative standard of poverty: an approach to defining poverty that sets the poverty level at a percentage of median income.

Representative sample: a small group selected from a totality in such a way as to be typical of the totality, so that conclusions drawn about the small group can be considered valid for the totality.

Social insurance: benefits based on recipients' work experience and funded by employer and/or employee contributions.

Social Security Act: the federal statute enacted in the 1930s that, as amended and expanded, establishes a wide range of federal social insurance and public assistance programs.

Social welfare programs: the programs through which a government addresses the needs of its least fortunate citizens.

Structural unemployment: joblessness caused by the inadequacies of job-seekers or by changes in the market for specific products.

Substandard housing: housing that (1) lacks essential facilities such as kitchens and/or bathrooms, or (2) is in visibly unsatisfactory physical condition.

Supplemental Security Income: a need-based income maintenance program that provides cash benefits to needy aged, blind, and disabled individuals.

Supported Work: a federal training program designed for groups deemed most difficult to serve and characterized by tightly structured work situations, peer support, and rigorous enforcement of rules.

Tax expenditure: a reduction in tax liability, authorized by legislation, that results in decreased government revenues.

Title I assistance: federal funds appropriated to school districts characterized by (1) high percentages of children from poor families (2) records of low student achievement.

Transfer payments: outlays by government for which no products are delivered or services rendered.

Underclass: a group within the urban ghetto poverty population characterized by long-term unemployment or withdrawal from the work force, criminal behavior, drug use, out-of-wedlock births, long-term welfare dependency.

Upper incomes: incomes substantially above the median income.

Veterans pensions: a cash transfer program that provides need-based benefits to veterans of wartime military service.

War on Poverty: the legislative effort launched in the 1960s to reduce poverty and ameliorate its effects.

WIC (Special Supplemental Food Program for Women, Infants, and Children): a federal social welfare program designed to ensure adequate nutrition for needy pregnant women, infants, and young children.

WIN (Work Incentive program): a program that attempted to get able-bodied AFDC recipients off the welfare rolls through education and training to make them employable.

Work effort: the extent to which an individual participates in the labor force.

Work experience: a type of training program in which participants are placed in subsidized private sector jobs to learn basic work habits rather than specific job skills.

Workfare: the practice of tying receipt of welfare benefits to performance of work by the recipients.

Working poor: those members of the labor force whose full-time work earns them incomes below the poverty level.

WPA (Works Progress Administration): the agency that headed a major job-creating program during the Great Depression.

Youth Incentive Entitlement Pilot Project: an attempt to keep potential dropouts in school and attract dropouts back to school by offering part-time jobs during the school year and full-time summer jobs.

NOTES

Chapter 1: Who Are the Poor?

1. U.S. Department of Commerce, Bureau of the Census, Current Population Reports, *Money Income and Poverty Status in the United States: 1988* (Advance Data From the March 1989 Current Population Survey), Consumer Income Series P-60, No. 166, 56.
2. ibid., 19.
3. Michael Morris and John B. Williamson, *Poverty and Public Policy: An Analysis of Federal Intervention Efforts* (New York: Greenwood Press, 1986), 14.
4. March 1989 Current Population Survey, 5.
5. ibid., 57.
6. ibid., 32.
7. All the data used to construct the graphs that follow in this chapter are from the March 1989 Current Population Survey.
8. Michael Novak, "The New War on Poverty," *Focus* (a periodical published by the University of Wisconsin–Madison Institute for Research on Poverty) (Spring 1988): 9.

Chapter 2: Sharpening the Picture of the Poor

1. Peter T. Kilborn, "Rise in Minimum Wage Offers Minimum Joy," *New York Times,* March 29, 1990, 1.
2. David T. Ellwood, *Poor Support: Poverty in the American Family* (New York: Basic Books, 1988), 87.
3. Sar A. Levitan and Elizabeth Conway, "Shortchanged by Part-Time Work," *New York Times,* February 27, 1988.
4. Kilborn, "Rise in Minimum Wage."
5. Robert J. Samuelson, "Help the Working Poor," *Newsweek,* May 1 1989, 52.
6. U.S. Library of Congress, Congressional Research Service, *Progress Against Poverty in the United States (1959 to 1987),* CRS Report for Congress, by Thomas Gabe, Report No. 89-211 EPW, 6.
7. *The Common Good: Social Welfare and the American Future,* Policy Recommendations of the Executive Panel (New York: Ford Foundation), May 1989, 56.
8. Editorial, "The Minimum Wage: A Distraction," *New York Times,* March 22, 1989, A26.
9. Myron Magnet, "America's Underclass: What To Do?," *Fortune,* May 11, 1987, 130.
10. ibid.
11. William Julius Wilson, *The Truly Disadvantaged: The Inner City, The Underclass, and Public Policy* (Chicago: The University of Chicago Press, 1987), 8.
12. Julie Johnson, "Blacks Found Lagging Despite Gains," *New York Times,* July 28, 1989, A6.
13. March 1989 Current Population Survey, 33.
14. Ellwood, *Poor Support,* 70.

Chapter 3: Income Maintenance Programs

1. U.S. Library of Congress, Congressional Research Service, CRS Report for Congress No. 89-595, *Cash and*

Noncash Benefits for Persons with Limited Income: Eligibility Rules, Recipient and Expenditure Data, FY 1986–88, October 24, 1989, 9.

2. Sheldon H. Danziger and Daniel H. Weinberg, eds., *Fighting Poverty: What Works and What Doesn't* (Cambridge, Mass.: Harvard University Press, 1986), 54.

3. CRS Report for Congress No. 89-595, *Summary* page.

4. ibid., 4.

5. Andrew Hacker, "Getting Rough on the Poor," *New York Review of Books,* October 13, 1988, 12.

6. CRS Report for Congress No. 89-595, 56.

7. ibid.

8. Sar A. Levitan and Isaac Shapiro, *Working But Poor: America's Contradiction* (Baltimore: Johns Hopkins University Press, 1987), 99.

9. Robert Moffitt, *Work and the U.S. Welfare System: A Review,* University of Wisconsin–Madison, Institute for Research on Poverty, Special Report Series #46, April 1988, 29.

10. ibid.

11. Moffitt, *Work and Welfare System,* 14.

12. CRS Report for Congress No. 89-595, 4.

13. Martin Tolchin, "Social Security Chief Seeks to Expand a U.S. Welfare Program, *New York Times,* December 29, 1989.

14. CRS Report for Congress No. 89-211, 14.

15. Tolchin, "Social Security Chief."

16. "The 1991 Budget: How $1.23 Trillion Would Be Distributed," Office of Management and Budget figures cited in *New York Times,* January 30, 1990, A21.

17. CRS Report for Congress No. 89-211, 19.

18. David E. Rosenbaum, "Prof. Moynihan Wakes the Class With Truth About Taxes," *New York Times,* January 21, 1990, E9.

Chapter 4: In-Kind Transfer Programs

1. Danziger and Weinberg, *Fighting Poverty*, 24.
2. Morris and Williamson, *Poverty and Public Policy*, 104.
3. Danziger and Weinberg, 388.
4. Morris and Williamson, 104.
5. CRS Report for Congress No. 89-595, 4.
6. ibid., 211.
7. U.S. Library of Congress, Congressional Research Service, CRS Report for Congress No. 89-196, *How the Food Stamp Program Works: 11th Edition*, by Joe Richardson, March 24, 1989, 68–69.
8. ibid., 61.
9. Robert Pear, "Many States Cut Food Allotments For Poor Families," *New York Times*, May 29, 1990, 1.
10. *A Decent Place to Live: The Report of the National Housing Task Force*, March 1988, 6.
11. CRS Report for Congress No. 89-595, 212.

Chapter 5: Investing in People: Education

1. Danziger and Weinberg, *Fighting Poverty*, 152.
2. ibid., 153.
3. ibid., 158.
4. Morris and Williamson, *Poverty and Public Policy*, 155.

Chapter 6: Investing in People: Training and Employment Programs

1. Danziger and Weinberg, *Fighting Poverty*, 171.
2. ibid.
3. "Luring Business: Joint South Jamaica Effort," *New York Times*, March 18, 1990, section 10, p. 1.
4. Morris and Williamson, p. 151.

Chapter 7: Welfare Reform I: Getting Tough with Absent Fathers

1. Mickey Kaus, "The Work Ethic State," *New Republic*, July 7, 1986, 24.

2. Robert E. Litan, Robert Z. Lawrence, and Charles L. Schultze, eds., *American Living Standards: Threats and Challenges* (Washington, D.C.: The Brookings Institution, 1988), 134.

3. Ellwood, *Poor Support,* 77.

4. Robert Haveman, *Starting Even: An Equal Opportunity Program to Combat the Nation's New Poverty,* A Twentieth Century Fund Report (New York: Simon and Schuster, 1988), 72.

5. Public Law 100-485, October 13, 1988, 102 STAT. 2343. Quoted in *Focus* (Winter 1988–1989): 15.

6. *Congressional Quarterly, Weekly Report,* June 18, 1988, 1648.

7. Ellwood, 159.

8. Hacker, "Getting Rough on the Poor," 13.

9. Michael deCourcy Hinds, "Better Traps Being Built For Delinquent Parents," *New York Times,* December 9, 1989, 11.

10. Ellwood, 165 ff.

Chapter 8: Welfare Reform II: Getting Young Mothers Off Welfare

1. Adapted from Michael deCourcy Hinds, "Pulling Families Out of Welfare Is Proving to Be an Elusive Goal," *New York Times,* April 2, 1990, 1.

2. Library of Congress, Congressional Research Service, CRS Report for Congress No. 88-702 EP, *The Family Support Act of 1988: How It Changes the Aid to Families with Dependent Children (AFDC) and Child Support Enforcement Programs,* by Carmen D. Solomon, November 6, 1988, 42.

3. Quoted in Julie Johnson, "Hopes for Welfare Program Clouded by Lack of Child Care," *New York Times,* December 12, 1989, A20.

4. U.S. Department of Commerce, Bureau of the Census, Current Population Reports, Household Economic

Studies Series P70 No. 9, *Who's Minding the Kids? Child Care Arrangements: Winter 1984–85,* 12.
5. Kaus, "The Work Ethic State," 29.
6. ibid., 27.
7. Hinds, "Pulling Families Out of Welfare," B8.

Chapter 9: The War That Is Not Over

1. Economic Opportunity Act of 1964, quoted in Hyman Bookbinder, "Did the War on Poverty Fail?", *New York Times,* August 20, 1989, E23.
2. Gary Burtless, "Public Spending for the Poor: Trends, Prospects, and Economic Limits," in Danziger and Weinberg, *Fighting Poverty,* 48.
3. Bookbinder, "Did the War on Poverty Fail?"
4. ibid.

FOR FURTHER READING

Coil, Suzanne. *The Poor in America*. New York: Messner, 1989.

Dudley, William. *Poverty*. San Diego: Greenhaven Press, 1988.

Kosof, Anna. *Homeless in America*. New York: Franklin Watts, 1988.

Meltzer, Milton. *Poverty in America*. New York: Morrow Junior Books, 1986.

INDEX

138

140

ABOUT THE AUTHOR

Bertha Davis holds a master's degree in economics from Columbia University and was a teacher and supervisor of social studies in the New York City school system for many years. She is an adjunct associate professor at New York University.

Among Ms. Davis's previous books for Franklin Watts are *Crisis in Industry: Can America Compete?*, *The National Debt,* and *Instead of Prison,* which *School Library Journal* praised as "a book [that] takes up where current periodicals leave off. . . . Davis, with expert advisers, has undertaken a heroic job of communicating an unresolved social problem." Ms. Davis's most recent book, *America's Housing Crisis,* was hailed by *School Library Journal* as "an excellent, much-needed book."

Ms. Davis lives with her husband in Cutchogue, New York.

Today, more than a quarter century after President John F. Kennedy's administration declared war on poverty, 6.9 million families—13.1 percent of the American population—still live in poverty. The existence of poverty in a nation with a long-standing image of wealth and opportunity is a glaring contradiction, and we must now ask the questions: How are we responding to the challenge that poverty continues to present? And what can the United States government and its citizens do about it?

In this book Bertha Davis uses the most up-to-date statistics to paint a sharp, sometimes startling, profile of America's poor. In the poverty population, whites outnumber blacks by better than two to one. Nearly 20 percent of people living below the poverty line are under eighteen years of age. Over half of the impoverished families in the nation are headed by women, with no spouse present.

With a keen grasp of complex social issues, Ms. Davis assesses major social welfare programs and describes specific policies to combat poverty, such as continually raising the employability of the poor, opening opportunities to the poor in the private-sector labor market, and creating public-service jobs. She also builds a case